A Genre Analysis of Social Change

Inkshed: Writing Studies in Canada

Series Editors
Roger Graves, University of Alberta
Heather Graves, University of Alberta

Inkshed Publications has published books on Canadian writing studies topics (broadly understood to include any of the interest areas described below) for twenty-five years. This new series formalizes that publication initiative. We seek to publish books that connect the work of writing studies scholars in Canada with the global writing studies community. We also want to engage with scholars throughout the world who want to connect their work with that done in Canada. Queries should be directed to the series editors: Roger Graves (graves1@ualberta.ca) and Heather Graves (hgraves@ualberta.ca).

INKSHED BOOKS

A Genre Analysis of Social Change: Uptake of the Housing-First Solution to Homelessness in Canada by Diana Wegner (2020)

Cross-Border Networks in Writing Studies by Derek Mueller, Andrea Williams, Louise Wetherbee Phelps, and Jennifer Clary-Lemon (2017).

Genre Studies around the Globe: Beyond the Three Tradition, edited by. Natasha Artemeva and Aviva Freedman (2015).

Writing in a Community of Practice: Composing Membership in Inkshed by Miriam Horne (2012).

Rhetorical Genre Studies and Beyond, edited by Natasha Artemeva and Aviva Freedman (2006).

Writing Centres, Writing Seminars, Writing Culture: Writing Instruction in Anglo-Canadian Universities, edited by Roger Graves and Heather Graves (2006).

Critical Moments in the Rhetoric of Kenneth Burke: Implications for Composition by Martin Behr (1996).

Integrating Visual and Verbal Literacies, by W. F. Garrett-Petts and Donald Lawrence (1996).

Writing Instruction in Canadian Universities by Roger Graves (1994).

Two Sides to a Story: Gender Difference in Student Narrative by Jaqueline McLeod Rogers (1994).

Contextual Literacy: Writing Across the Curriculum, edited by Catherine F. Schryer and Laurence Steven Jaqueline McLeod Rogers (1994).

A GENRE ANALYSIS OF SOCIAL CHANGE

Uptake of the Housing-First Solution to
Homelessness in Canada

Diana Wegner

Parlor Press
Anderson, South Carolina
www.parlorpress.com

Parlor Press LLC, Anderson, South Carolina, USA
Printed in the United States of America on acid-free paper.

S A N: 2 5 4 - 8 8 7 9

Library of Congress Cataloging-in-Publication Data on File

Names: Wegner, Diana, 1949- author.
Title: A genre analysis of social change : uptake of the housing-first   solution to homelessness in Canada / Diana Wegner.
Description: Anderson, South Caroliuna : Parlor Press, [2021] | Series:
Inkshed: writing studies in Canada | Includes bibliographical references.
| Summary: "Contributes to scholarship in genre studies and discourse
analysis in contexts of social change. Wegner shows how systems of genre
adapt to change as groups and institutions struggle across genres and
their spheres of activities over the "uptake" of solutions to social challenges, specifically the "Housing First" solution to homelessness"-- Provided
by publisher.
Identifiers: LCCN 2021026637 (print) | LCCN 2021026638 (ebook) |
ISBN 9781643171791 (paperback) | ISBN 9781643171807 (pdf) | ISBN
9781643171814 (epub)
Subjects: LCSH: Homelessness--Canada. | Discourse analysis. | Social
change--Canada.
Classification: LCC HV4509 .W44 2021 (print) | LCC HV4509 (ebook) |
DDC 362.5/920971--dc23
LC record available at https://lccn.loc.gov/2021026637
LC ebook record available at https://lccn.loc.gov/2021026638

2 3 4 5

Cover design by David Blakesley.
Cover image created by Fernando Cobelo. Submitted for United Nations
Global Call Out to Creatives. Unsplash.com

Parlor Press, LLC is an independent publisher of scholarly and trade titles in
print and multimedia formats. This book is available in paper and ebook formats from Parlor Press on the World Wide Web at http://www.parlorpress.
com or through online and brick-and-mortar bookstores. For submission information or to find out about Parlor Press publications, write to Parlor Press,
3015 Brackenberry Drive, Anderson, South Carolina, 29621, or email edi-
tor@parlorpress.com.

Contents

Series Editor's Introduction

Heather Graves

Since the 1990s, researchers have produced a small but continuing body of scholarship that probes and attenuates theories of discourse in the context of homelessness, not only in Canada but also in the US and Europe. Three general streams of analysis have emerged from these studies: self-representations of homelessness, media representations of homelessness, and institutional discourse on the issue of homelessness. Those studies examining self-representations have looked primarily at homeless blogs. In Canada, Grafton and Maurer (2007) have studied the genre-based phenomenon of uptake in self-cultivation and validation in bloggers' postings associated with the Canada Reads event and homelessness. Schneider (2012a) has also studied blogging in the homeless community as part of a larger study on media representations of the homeless (2012b; Schneider, Chamberlain & Hodgetts, 2010). This earlier work on blog postings investigated how these writers engaged public audiences to first describe and explore but then ultimately influence their situations.

A second line of inquiry focuses on representations of homeless people in media genres, such as street newspapers, mainstream newspapers, and documentary film. Torck (2001) analyzes four street newspapers (two from Europe, one from the UK and one from the US) and reports that they published more articles *about* homeless people than *by* them. She notes that the newspapers portray homeless individuals as caricatures or infantilize them, and the editors restrict the genres available to the homeless writers they did publish to the expressive or emotional such as poetry or autobiography. Huckin (2002) examines a large corpus of newspaper articles to illustrate how manipulative textual silence, the fourth in his taxonomy of textual silences, was used in newspaper articles to misrepresent and diminish homeless people in the eyes of readers. Loehwing

(2010, p. 382) analyzes the documentary, *Reversal of Fortune*, and concludes that it served to set up its protagonist, Ted Rodrigue, for failure by reinforcing what she calls a "present-centredness" that characterizes homelessness as "the inability to escape a perpetual 'focus upon passions, desires, and appetites'" that forestalls pursuing long-term projects that would end the individual's homeless situation. Interestingly, much of this scholarship on the discourse of homelessness reveals that the rhetoric of homelessness and the discursive treatment of the homeless, while ostensibly seeking solutions, in fact perpetuate an ideology that 1) prevents effective solutions, or 2) reduces the chances an effective solution might be successful.

A third stream of study has focused on institutional discourse and genres deployed in the homelessness genre system. Diana Wegner's study takes this perspective, contributing to our knowledge in the Canadian context. Her study aligns with research in Europe that examines public and institutional discourse about homelessness, including how different genres and their participants define and characterize homelessness. Aragpoglou (2004a, 2004b), particularly, has focused on how "power and culture," as expressed through the institutional genres of governance, advocacy and social services "produce segmented responses to homelessness in the European South" (2004a, p. 631). He found that narrow definitions of homelessness in dominant institutional genres are used to mark individuals "who deserve pity" and exclude those "who did not deserve pity," (2004b, p. 119) including immigrants, drug addicts, the mentally ill, criminals and people just released from prison. In his study, for example, this limiting definition reduced the 'homeless' population in Athens from 100,000+ to a few hundred, making it a problem that was easily 'solved' (2004b).

This volume contributes to current scholarship on institutional discourses and genres associated with homelessness but adds a new dimension to the conversation by exploring the ways that historical genre systems can be transformed through the process of governmental uptake. It represents the summation of Wegner's work over many years on how systems of genre change and can evolve as groups and institutional systems struggle to find solutions to major social challenges. She has focused particularly on this process as it has been manifested in a Canadian version of the discourse on homelessness, specifically the "Housing First" (HF) solution to homelessness as implemented in Greater Vancouver, British Columbia (BC), from 2010 - 2015. The historical version of HF entails the immediate housing of homeless people with no qualifying criteria, after which they are provided with a full set of wrap-around services of their own choosing. She studied a series of sites to explore the pathways by which the Housing-First approach to homelessness influenced or was taken up into municipal (Vancouver and suburbs), provincial (B.C.), and federal genres of Canadian governance. This monograph is based on her exploration and analysis of how the HF approach was applied in these contexts with the goal of contributing to the further development of this concept of taking up or 'uptake' in rhetorical genre studies. She focuses specifically on the dynamics of uptake across genres and genre systems and how rhetorical genre analysis can offer insight into issues related to social justice for marginal groups within society.

Wegner has had a long-standing interest in the struggles of homeless people and in municipal attention and conversations about addressing the need to house this population. This project began in response to the prevalence of public discourse in 2010 about "the homeless problem" in the Vancouver area, as the city prepared to host the winter Olympics, and then followed ongoing discussions about how to 'solve' homelessness. She initially searched for the presence of homeless people and their housing in municipal genres in British Columbia and, after finding them absent in official genres such as Official Community Plans, turned to the level of advocacy, which brought her to the study of the genre of municipal Housing and Homelessness Strategic Plans (HSPs). The advocates who she observed and interviewed were focused on the HF approach to homelessness, which led Wegner to explore the process and instantiation of HF uptake from its early emergence in the U.S. in the genre of 10 year strategic plans to its implementation in Canada. She aimed to study the phenomenon of HF to examine how advocacy and more powerful groups—primarily government, but also media and certain publics, both clashed and cooperated in the struggle to address lack of housing for the homeless and, through this examination, to elucidate the roles of genre, uptake, and memory in this process. These three interrelated concepts—genre, uptake and memory—are key terms in Wegner's work.

Genre: The activity of addressing or 'solving' a social problem is a discursive process, characterized by the deployment of socially recognized entities or "genres," both written and spoken. In the homelessness genre system these included official community plans, housing strategic plans, research reports, legislation, policy, requests for proposals, funding applications, and task force meetings. Genres offer communities shared, recurrent forms as blueprints and resources for addressing recurrent social situations—they are crucial verbal means for addressing social issues and, as such, genres invariably interact with each other. For example, in Wegner's study, genre participants strategize to offer HF uptake from housing strategic plans, advocacy reports, and first-hand experience, to the research community. Subsequently, the findings from research—uptake from advocacy—lead to new federal legislation, which in turn leads to the selection of successful funding applications, albeit for a limited number of service-providers, and finally to the implementation of change in the social and material worlds of advocates and homeless individuals. Together, the genres that constitute these systems can ultimately alter the nature of the interactions between government, advocacy groups and the homeless people they serve. As these multiple discursive uptakes from one genre system cross over into another, genres can influence each other in potentially transformative ways.

Uptake: The genre-based concept of uptake is dialogical and multi-directional, and often produces mixed results, reflecting different motivations among genre participants. Uptake always entails the activation of situational and textual elements of both the original genre and the uptake genre. The mix is often unpredictable. The possibility that uptake from one genre into another may lead to social change elsewhere in the system exists, but is not inevitable. Uptake of a discursive entity from one genre into another can occur routinely, serendipitously, or strategically, as the producers of one discursive entity encounter and recognize the usefulness of another. In the most rhetorically fitting cases, this uptake preserves critical features of the original discursive entity that positively contribute or even energize the uptake genre where it is recontextualized. However, in other cases where participants may be unaware of or ignore the original context and purpose of a genre, in their effort to shape the repurposed discursive entity to fit *their* context, uptake can become infelicitous. Even as it alters its new context, its historical elements can come into conflict with unintended effects of recontextualization.

The concept of uptake emerged in rhetorical genre studies after Freadman (1987) appropriated it from Austin's speech act theory (1962) and re-theorized it for genre studies. Freadman (2002, p.

40) defines uptake as "the bi-directional relation [between] a pair of texts." It is a social interaction and frequently involves power relations. Uptake has therefore been applied in analyses of rhetorical strategy (Freadman, 1987, 2002, 2012; Devitt, 2009) and, in particular, in the exploration of the dynamics and effects of power relations (Emmons, 2009; Freadman, 2002; Tachino, 2012). These studies have postulated uptake as boundary crossing or "translation" (Freadman, 2002, p. 43): in the context of asymmetrical power relations uptake can be accepted, refused or resisted by members of one genre system in response to members of another system.

While these studies explore rhetorical motivation and strategy and the dynamics of power relations, they do not expressly describe or problematize the relationship between genre and uptake. In Wegner's study, she probes the nature of this relationship to elaborate uptake as a theoretical concept and to assess to what extent a genre framework is productive or even necessary for analyses of uptake.

Memory: The third key term in Wegner's analysis is memory, derived from the insight that although a genre is transformed following uptake, residual elements of the original persist as "genre memory" within the new genre. For example, in her study of HF, when government policy incorporated the HF approach into its funding criteria, it adopted a version of HF that prioritizes service to the mentally ill and chronically homeless and excludes other homeless populations. However, the original HF intent was characterized by its strong bent towards social justice and inclusiveness, a fact that policy writers either overlooked or were ignorant of, but that, as Wegner shows, is embedded in advocacy genres and discourse. She shows how homelessness advocacy groups, who have been historically motivated in their work by the belief that housing is a human right, prize inclusiveness and aim to serve hidden homeless populations that, for example, also include women and families. This value of inclusiveness sets the advocacy groups that she studied in conflict with the new legislation and its funding eligibility criteria that excludes significant groups by its focus on the chronically homeless. The advocates' response to the legislative criteria for HF funding was to resist its narrow focus by findings ways to implement it inclusively. Wegner argues that genre 'memory' motivated advocacy groups to pressure government to moderate its new vision of HF to incorporate what they felt were essential elements of the original version—advocates perceived where government policy fell short and responded by foregrounding what was still present as memory in the genre system but lost in the process of government taking up the HF approach to homelessness.

Using a genre theory framework, Wegner traces a series of uptakes of the HF approach to homelessness in the Canadian context (2010-2015) where, as noted, HF funding criteria significantly changed eligibility for receiving federal homelessness funds. She analyses these multiple uptakes of HF and probes the relationship between genre and uptake to explain the dynamics of struggle and advocacy wherein participants in the homelessness genre system interpret and reinterpret HF as it crosses from genre to genre. She tracks how genre has effects at the level of phraseology by following the trajectories of "uptake artifacts" or "texts that respond to other texts" (Dryer, 2012), and the effects of "genre residue" or memory—that which adheres to language when it is imported from one textual context into another new one. The concept of "genre memory" (Bakhtin, 1963) helps explain how, as uptake crosses boundaries from one genre to another, obvious omissions of salient elements from the previous generic context into the new one might profoundly disturb veteran participants in the homelessness genre system. Since uptake involves the movement across texts/genres of a "coupling of forms and content, as well as coupling of language, social action, and power relationship[s]" (Tachino, 2013, p. 4), as it resituates discursive formations in another genre/context, it brings with it the generic "memory" of its former meaning, context, and power relations; these new text/context couplings, in turn, become the conditions of possibility for ongoing struggle and rhetorical strategy, thereby furnishing affordances for further uptake.

In this study, as uptake of the HF model crosses over from advocacy into the higher-level, more official, powerful genres of research and governance, advocates respond to both uptake presences and absences with their own uptake strategies and historically-based understandings of the HF legislation. Wegner addresses these questions:

- What genre dynamics are at play?
- How does HF uptake as "generic translation" explain what happens to the traditional practices of homeless services?
- What can a rhetorical genre approach reveal of what is often obscure in the movement of uptake?

• What linguistic evidence can it bring forth to illuminate the power relations at work in enduring struggles like homelessness?

To answer these questions, she extends the discussion of the role of genre theory in explanatory accounts of uptake as a concept and as a strategy.

Overall, the findings of this study suggest that well-worn pathways across genres can facilitate deep uptake; however, unusual or foreign pathways across genres can foster uptake that is shallow and potentially problematic. In this study, the uptake of the HF model from advocacy genres into municipal homelessness strategic plans follows pathways that are well worn, and consequently, the genres tend to be historically shared, facilitated and supported. In contrast, uptake by provincial/state government that created new funding criteria based on its problematic understanding of the HF approach represents an uptake pathway that is unexpected or unusual. In this case, uptake is problematic and disturbing for those participants in the homelessness genre system who find that the receiving genre does not "remember" the historical moorings of its antecedent contexts. Genre provides an explanatory framework for these uptake dynamics and for the discursive dimension of struggle. In terms of homelessness and social justice, the change in government policy to a HF approach has had two effects. The new policy both excludes many people at-risk of homelessness and includes populations for whom the costly HF approach is neither feasible nor appropriate. Both these outcomes violate the genre memory of participants in the homelessness system in terms of who should be included in HF programs. As a result, instead of embracing the federal HF model, many service providers in BC have resisted and criticized its implementation, even as they acquiesce to the new criteria in their funding proposals.

Findings elsewhere indicate that local resistance to how the HF model has been taken up and interpreted by government is not an isolated phenomenon. Such criticism and a re-thinking of the HF approach has affected recent policy in Great Britain and the EU. The "paradigm shift" in Canada to a HF model that targets only the most chronic of homeless populations is now giving way elsewhere to "paradigm drift" (Pleace & Bretherton, n.d.) whereby serious consideration is given to broadened versions and variants of the original Pathways HF model. These variants are, in part, a response to its exclusionary emphasis, as seen in critiques of its focus on the most chronic and visible homeless. Wegner finds these critiques issue from the deep genre memory of homelessness advocates as a challenge to what they see as egregious absences in the federal government's uptake of a misguided and problematic version of HF. Such uptake, she argues, is informed by a shallow genre memory of HF and insufficient participant history in the Canadian homelessness genre system, an explanation that she anchors productively within a genre theory framework.

Wegner's analysis of genre dynamics and uptake is important on three levels. It illuminates this case study of inept government policy change, motivated by a desire to do the right thing but not commit the resources to ensure the change achieves success. Wegner traces how the provincial government made a good faith effort to address homelessness but its policy to implement its version of the HF solution was problematic for participants due to the partial uptake of the HF model from research genres into governance. The policy-makers cherry-picked affordable elements from the successful Canadian pilot version of HF and ignored key supporting programs that enabled its success. They then implemented the truncated version without regard for how or even whether the new policy integrated with the existing system. Consequently, advocacy groups whose existing programs responded to funding criteria from the legacy system were unable to qualify for the new HF funds; as a result, many homeless people were excluded from the new narrowed definition of who qualified for the HF program.

Second, Wegner extends existing genre theory in two areas: the concepts of uptake, both routine and disruptive, and genre memory, which in her study she identifies as an antidote to disruptive uptake. Wegner traces how uptake unfolds in the context of the asymmetrical power relations between provincial government legislation and advocacy groups working with the homeless. Some of this uptake proved to be routine and non-problematic, such as the uptake of ideas about HF into lower level genres of policy (such as housing strategic plans) or the impact on research of HF as implemented by advocacy groups. Other uptake, however, became problematic and disruptive when, for example, research on HF was taken up by government and transformed into policy and then funding criteria. Wegner then traces how subsequent uptake by advocacy groups of the new government policy/funding criteria resulted in some resistance but also constructive responses where genre memory shaped how the policy was implemented.

Wegner distinguishes two types of genre memory: a shallow, fossilized genre memory and a deep, active genre memory. She argues that the government's uptake of HF research that it transformed into policy and new funding criteria drew on the former type, shallow and fossilized. She notes that this type was a consequence of taking up the form of the genre but casting aside its historical context. In contrast, advocacy groups charged with meeting the new funding criteria drew on a deep, active genre memory that retained its historical context. This active genre memory allowed advocacy groups to devise strategies to mitigate the restrictions of the new criteria and to work together to fulfill their collective mandate to serve homeless people in their communities.

A significant finding of Wegner's study is that there is value to understanding uptake as a genre-based phenomenon. Her analysis shows how uptake is multiple, contingent, and jointly mediated, in this case, by government, researchers, and advocacy groups. She further emphasizes that genre-crossing is, in fact, a dialogical encounter of past and present, and the residue remaining from previous genres can be shallow or deep. Finally, Wegner's study illustrates how uptake, in the case of HF in British Columbia (Canada), was a series of joint mediations between government and advocacy groups. Their discursive interactions served to re-inscribe their power relations while simultaneously making incremental progress on their shared struggle to help homeless people in British Columbia

REFERENCES

Arapoglou, V. (2004a). "The Governance of Homelessness in the European South: Spatial and Institutional Contexts of Philanthropy in Athens." *Urban Studies 41*(3), 621–639.

Arapoglou, V. (2004b). "The Governance of Homelessness in Greece: discourse and power in the study of philanthropic networks." *Critical Social Policy 24*(1), 102–126.

Chowers, E. (2002). "The Physiology of the Citizen: The Present-Centred Body and Its Political Exile." *Political Theory 30*, 649–676. Cited in Loehwing, M. (2010). "Homelessness as the Unforgiving Minute of the Present: The Rhetorical Tenses of Democratic Citizenship." *Quarterly Journal of Speech 96*(4), 380–403.

Grafton, K, & Maurer, E. (2007, August 16). "Public Engagements and public arrangements of blog genres." Proceedings of the 4th International

Symposium on Genre Studies, August 15–18, 2007, 164–174. University of Southern Santa Catarina. Tubarao, Brazil. http://www3.unisul.br/paginas/ensino/pos/linguagem/cd/English/17i.pdf

Huckin, T. (2002). "Textual Silence and the discourse of homelessness." *Discourse & Society 13*(3), 347–372.

Loehwing, M. (2010). "Homelessness as the Unforgiving Minute of the Present: The Rhetorical Tenses of Democratic Citizenship." *Quarterly Journal of Speech 96*(4), 380–403.

Schneider, B. (2012). "Blogging Homelessness: Technology of the Self or Practice of Freedom?" *Canadian Journal of Communication 37*, 405–419.

Schneider, B., Chamberlain, K., & Hodgetts, D. (2010). Representations of homelessness in four Canadian newspapers: Regulation, control, and social order. *Journal of sociology & Social Welfare, 37*(4), 147–172.

Torck, D. (2001). "Voices of Homeless People in Street Newspapers: A Cross-Cultural Exploration. *Discourse and Society 12*(3)

Glossary

ACT	Assertive Community Treatment
AH/SC	At Home/Chez Soi research project
CAEH	Canadian Alliance to End Homelessness
EFry	Elizabeth Fry
HF	Housing First
HPS	Housing Partnering Strategy
HSP	Housing and Homelessness Strategic Plan
MHCC	Mental Health Commission of Canada
OCP	Official Community Plan
PHF	Pathways Housing First
RSCH	Regional Steering Committee on Homelessness (Metro-Vancouver)

A Genre Analysis of Social Change

1 Uptake and Genre

Homelessness Task Force Member: "I look forward to seeing your magic."

Housing-First Project Manager: "I also look forward to it. I believe in magic. So. [laughter] We'll see." (Housing and Homelessness Task Force Meeting, Municipality 2, April 28/2015)

* * *

Speaker 1: I don't know if any [of you] have heard of the At-Home project in Vancouver but it's a federally funded [Housing-First demonstration project]. . . . The whole concept of what we do is that it's a housing-first model . . . we guarantee the rent. . . . we can't kick people out . . . Housing to our mind is a form of therapy.

Speaker 2: It's the housing-first model.

Speaker 1: It's the housing-first model. It is a form of therapy. Just having the housing itself . . . (Homelessness Task Force Meeting, Municipality 1, Feb. 1/2013)

* * *

It [Housing First] has ... been heralded as presenting a key "antidote" to chronic homelessness and is being replicated across North America and Europe with what might be regarded as "evangelical" fervour. (Johnsen and Teixiera, 2012, p. 183)

At first, the homelessness advocacy community embraced the federal government's adoption of the Housing First (HF) model, but this euphoria quickly turned to dismay. Their response to new legislation revealed critical differences between these two jurisdictions in collective memories, cultures, and practices. To meet their social justice goals within the HF eligibility constraints imposed by the government, advocates mou nted their own strategic retranslation of Housing First. The following analysis of the successive uptakes of HF across different jurisdictions, including the research community, is intended to illuminate both its non-problematic and disruptive effects. It is intended to provide insights into the missteps of a government that imposed a politically opportunistic solution to a social problem and the resistance and strategy of a marginal community responding to this imposition.

In rhetorical genre studies, the concept of uptake (Freadman, 1987, 2002, 2012; Devitt, 2009) has been developed and applied to describe and explain the dynamics—motivations and strategies—set into play when discursive entities cross genre boundaries (Bawarshi, 2016; Emmons, 2009; Freadman, 1987/1994, 2002; Giltrow, 2016; Tachino, 2016, 2013). For example, Emmons (2009) follows a list of symptoms as it migrates from the DSM onto the internet as a "do-it-yourself" set of diagnostic questions; Freadman (2002) shows how a judge's death sentence is transposed into the realm of politics and becomes an execution; Tachino (2013, 2016) tracks a finding from research that becomes evidence in a public inquiry. Such studies have led theorists to postulate a description of uptake as "movement" and "translation" (Freadman, 2002, p. 43) of discursive entities, both textual and contextual, across genres, sometimes in routine ways (recommendations from management become policy) and sometimes more strategically (a private complaint becomes an investigative report). The concept of uptake has been useful for shedding light on rhetorical motivation and strategy and on the dynamics of power relations as different genres come into contact with each other through the selection of particular uptakes. In this study, as research and advocacy are put into contact with governance genres, the findings from studies of supportive housing for certain homeless populations are promoted by advocacy at the political level and translated by the government into funding for a specific social housing model, Housing First.

Recent scholarship has invited closer scrutiny of the concept of uptake, with researchers like Dryer (2012) inviting genre theorists to refine our understanding of uptake and to problematize the relationship between genre and uptake. Until recently genre studies has tended to work with "stable" models of genre, as recurrent cultural practices and artefacts, most notably in Education, for example, in studies of English for Specific Purposes (Hyland, 1999 and 2009). However, with Freadman's (2012) emphasis on the "destabilizing" effects of uptake on genre (p. 560), and Schryer's thesis (1993) that genres are only ever "stabilized for now" (p. 208), genre theorists have turned their attention to contingencies of uptake and genre. Bawarshi (2016) probes "genre memory" and the "historical -material conditions" of uptake and genre that "hold" power relations in place (p. 52). Giltrow (2016) has introduced the concept of "mutual consciousness" into genre theory as the repository of tacit shared knowledge and an explanation for uptake "silences" that destabilize genre by eliding context or certain "consciousnesses" in favour of "form alone" (pp. 220-221). Dryer (2016) proposes a taxonomy of five kinds of uptake for a more incisive lens on how it functions in relation to genre, and offers an important critique of unconscious, almost automatic, uptake of certain discursive entities that he argues should be held at arm's length and examined first. And Tachino (2016) situates uptake "at a nexus of multiple and (possibly competing) intertextual threads" activated or drawn from a range of genres, each oriented differently to an exigence. He frames this uptake activity within a network of genres and genre "residue" (Spinuzzi, 2003), using the contextual concept of a "genre ecology" (Spinuzzi and Zachry, 2000), whose activated generic threads "jointly mediate" social action (pp. 181-182).

This study aims to build upon these contributions to probe the relationship between uptake and genre to elaborate the historical dimension of genre, its "memory," and its role in uptake enactments, whether the effects are non-problematic, disruptive, or constructive. Why do certain discursive threads come into play? How this does "play" and mediation explain the effects of uptake? What happens when genre memory is confirmed, when it is violated, when it is retrieved? This probing of genre and uptake is undertaken by analyzing an interdiscursive chain of uptake. It follows a series of uptakes for evidence of participant memory (as shared knowledge) and traces of "genre residue" to pursue which generic threads are put into play, what happens in uptake enactment—the material realization of the act of selecting a particular bundle of uptake threads from the sphere of advocacy activity for language in policy and budgetary genres. It examines the effects that these enactments have, and what uptakes, in turn, are selected by participants in response to policy and funding uptake. This study contributes to current theorizing of the contextual dimension of genre that is "genre memory" and shows how it is both a motivation and an effect of uptake as a process of "joint mediation" of multiple generic threads. To this end, I distinguish between active, deep genre memory (that of veteran activists in the homelessness advocacy community) and fossilized, shallow genre memory (that of those non-members of the advocacy community such as politicians and researchers) for its usefulness in explaining the countervailing effects of generic uptake. Such uptake involves the "joint mediation" of advocacy, research and governance genres that is both disruptive and re-stabilizing. In applying a memory-based analysis of uptake and genre to a charged social issue, I show how such analyses can help us understand the effects of contingency and unpredictability through disruptive uptake enactments in processes of social change. This entails exploring the differences between types of uptake—characterized in this study as unproblematic (routine adoption of task force recommendations into municipal strategic plans), disruptive (new HF legislation that disrupts historical practices embedded in the advocacy community), and constructive (strategic adaptations of HF by advocates and service-providers). This exploration reveals how the front stages of dominant power (government bolstered by mainstream media) can veil its disruptive effects on the less powerful in the backstages of struggle (in the operations of shelters, recovery houses, and social services). It also reveals how cooperative uptake between the two can move an issue forward.

This investigation of the relationship between genre and uptake is pursued in the arena of homelessness discourse and the "enduring struggle" (Lave and Wenger, 2001) of advocacy for homeless people. Specifically, the study traces the historical conditions that led to a series of uptakes of the "Housing-First" (HF) approach to homelessness in the Canadian context. The original "Pathways" version of HF (1990s) (PHF) stipulates the immediate housing of "chronically and episodically" homeless people with no qualifying criteria, after which they are provided with a full set of wrap-around support services of their own choosing. Over the last 30 years, however, the homelessness advocacy community has undergone subtle but significant changes towards greater inclusiveness and flexibility in its philosophy of HF and how to approach homelessness.

These changes have become shared knowledge among participants in the advocacy genre system and inhabit that sphere of activity as both textual and tacit genre memory. This study traces HF incarnations through the examination of a discursive chain of key uptake enactments, each with attendant genre assumptions, expectations, and memory. Each is propelled by the complex and varying motivations and strategies of genre participants who select interdiscursive threads from available genre affordances, translating and re-translating HF within the homelessness genre system. This system is a sphere of activity that includes core participants (advocates, outreach workers, service-providers of housing, health, and social services, law enforcement, legal aid, homeless people), more peripheral actors (researchers, relevant government departments, the media), and core genres (press releases, strategic plans, task force meetings, and homeless counts). The analysis ends with a description of the social action this discursive chain has accomplished. This chain includes the most recent uptake of HF, in the form of improvised strategies that produce diverse material realizations of HF—unique, localized housing sites for homeless people.

In brief, using a rhetorical genre framework, recent theorizing of uptake, and a Foucauldian sensibility toward institutional power in terms of how power relations circulate among dominant and marginal groups, the analyses in this book trace the history and contexts of the HF philosophy: its adoption from advocacy into policy and research, from research and advocacy into legislation (the 2013 federal budget), and from federal HF funding criteria into implementation by advocates and service-providers. These analyses of rhetorical strategy and uptake across genre boundaries are applied in the context of evolving understandings of HF within the homelessness genre system, especially in the advocacy community. The discursive chain includes idealized early versions of HF with currency in the advocacy community, the federal government's cost-effective version, and the more recent adaptive, flexible versions based on the realities of limited funding and support for homeless people and their local needs.

Overall, findings show that, not surprisingly, official, high-level genres in the homelessness genre system tend to block robust HF uptake from advocacy and research, but also that the same system affords joint mediation of generic threads as a "kairotic coordination of social action" by stakeholders (Yates and Orlikowski, 2002). Specifically, HF uptake enactment from research into legislation, a high-level governance genre, delimited and narrowed the scope of homelessness funding. In response, advocates exploited available genre affordances in HF uptake toward a broader, more inclusive, and compensatory implementation of HF. The findings show that the role of genre memory is significant in these uptake enactments and their effects. It is particularly evident in participants' memory of the historical evolution of the value of inclusivity whereby they have come to see their advocacy as encompassing all people who are homeless, a value that advocacy discourse absorbed from human rights discourse. An inclusive list of homeless people, both the chronically homeless and those at risk of homelessness, and their respective needs, has persisted in the genre system as deep genre memory and residue, and this shared memory animates and perpetuates the struggle for the homeless. As advocates, in turn, took up the federal HF funding criteria, they deployed their traditional practices of collaboration, to develop successful HF proposals, and, then, to work towards inclusive implementations of HF sites.

These findings suggest that some intended uptakes are secured un-problematically, especially when facilitated by the historical and mutual investment of values and practices by participants. For example, municipal task forces have taken up the endorsement of HF and an expand-ed inclusive list of at-risk categories of homeless people from advocacy genres into municipal homelessness strategic plans. In other cases, even when uptake is facilitated by a routine, intermediary genre, where there is a lack of historical and mutual alignment of values, where one genre does not "remember" the historical moorings of antecedent genres, in-tended uptake can be secured but with problematic effects. For example, the enactment of HF uptake from research into legislation results in a significant disturbance in the genre system of advocacy, a disturbance that is corroborated by HF scholarship that reappraises and critiques governments that promote and favour the PHF model for their misguid-ed policy "overreach" (Kertesz et al., 2009).

This monograph incorporates current developments in studies of up-take and genre, specifically the role of genre memory and genre con-sciousness, and the process and effects of uptake enactments. I also propose a distinction between "deep," shared memory, and "shallow" memory, a lack of shared memory, to help explain how uptake across genre boundaries can disrupt and destabilize genre. An analysis of the HF uptake chain shows it has activated genre residue, both fossilized PHF residue (shallow, "inert" genre memory) appealing to the government, and reinvigorated residue of the value of inclusivity and care and a history of shared struggle (deep genre memory) among advocates. On the one hand, advocates have come to embrace an inclusive philosophy that has evolved in tandem with changes and adaptations to both HF and non-HF approaches to homelessness. As recent policy studies show, many models based on HF do not show strict fidelity to all its original principles in their real implementation (Pleace and Bretherton, 2012). On the other hand, the federal government has not, apparently, attended to these evolving understandings in the advocacy community but has, instead, adopted its understanding of HF from fossilized residue from the early days of PHF, replicated in its At Home/*Chez Soi* HF research project, and subsequently in its 2013 legislation. Notably, the PHF version had been replicated in legislation by other western countries and has now been the object of policy critiques.

Through an application of the analytical concepts of genre memory, genre residue, genre affordances, genre practices, and uptake, this study foregrounds how the contextual dimension of genre constitutes the social action it accomplishes. As uptake encounters a genre boundary, it carries a genre'd memory that affects the uptake genre; in turn, the uptake genre influences how uptake becomes resituated. The effects are both disruptive and (re)stabilizing. As in Tachino's study of the preliminary inquiry (2016), HF uptake is shown to be multiply-directional, unpredictable, yet stabilized-for-now by the re-organizing contextual forces that result in a unique generic fusion and a generically recognizable social action.

BACKGROUND: HOUSING FIRST AND THE FEDERAL GOVERNMENT

In Canada, homelessness funding policy has been influenced through uptake from both popularized notions of the causes of homelessness that can generate both public sympathy and social stigma, and from the lobbying efforts of homelessness advocacy groups. Policy decisions about homelessness funding eligibility criteria, both HF and non-HF, have, in turn, driven how service providers have responded with their own uptake. Until a few decades ago, the traditional emphasis in funding and advocacy had been on treatment-first (the continuum-of-care model that makes treatment a prerequisite for housing), and not housing-first (as a perquisite to recovery). Homelessness advocates have developed a wide variety of categories of homeless populations that should be eligible for support services, crucially including not just the chronically homeless, but also those "at-risk" of homelessness. Traditionally, certain homeless and at-risk categories (those the public and media are sympathetic towards) have been eligible for targeted services for their needs: not only "the chronically and episodically homeless" (e.g., the mentally ill, and drug-addicted—the street homeless), but also some populations at-risk of homelessness (e.g., single mothers, youth, seniors).

In Canada, since 2013, the HF model has, in effect, supplanted the traditional "services" model. As the number of homeless and at-risk people in Canada has grown over the last 30 years, advocacy and news coverage have intensified, and homelessness research and policy have responded, most recently, in 2013, with the adoption of the HF model into Canadian federal legislation and funding (the Housing Partnering Strategy or HPS). This legislation follows uptake from the results of a government-sponsored HF research project, At Home/*Chez Soi* (AH/CS):

> [Canada's] Economic Action Plan 2013 proposes $119 million per year over five years ... to the Homelessness Partnering Strategy using a "Housing First" approach. The outcomes of the Mental Health Commission of Canada's At Home/Chez Soi Project have shown that providing *Housing First* ... [is] an effective way to reduce homelessness. (Homelessness Partnering Strategy, Ch. 3.5: Supporting Families and Communities, *Budget 2013*, Government of Canada, March 21/13).

The funding criteria correspondingly underwent significant change, with unprecedented emphasis on "barrier-free" entry into "housing-first" or "permanent housing" projects targeting chronically and episodically homeless people. The change occurred primarily because of the high costs this group incurs for health, law enforcement, justice, and social services. As a result, federal homelessness funding was redirected away from homelessness *services* for both chronically episodically homeless and at-risk populations to *HF projects* for the chronically and episodically homeless (65% of the fund), such that permanent housing projects with full support services and "no barrier" entry criteria were now favoured for funding over non-HF services. In the past, the situation had been reversed, so that many non-HF service providers who worked with various categories of homeless populations who were previously eligible for funding had to compete for the remaining 35% of the budget. In the province of British Columbia, the change in funding priorities, despite being championed by many homelessness advocates, initially challenged and undermined the structure of the homeless service-provider sector. After this jolt of change registered, however, advocates and service-providers responded by working together to meet both the government's HF criteria and advocacy priorities, capitalizing on genre opportunities or "affordances" in their community toward the goal of inclusivity.

This study specifically pursues uptake of the discursive life of two generic entities of advocacy across genres: 1) the HF approach to homelessness and 2) the recurring inclusive list of categories of homeless people in the context of advocacy and governance. As noted, uptake of the HF approach is followed through its re-interpretations by advocates, researchers, policy analysts, and government, into its adoption in the March 2013 federal budget, and subsequently, by advocates and service-providers responding to the government's uptake of HF. It pursues uptake's role in both genre disruption and genre reorganization in the context of asymmetrical power relations. It treats genre as both a resource for uptake affordances and a set of constraints that become flashpoints for transformation as uptake crosses from one genre to another. Manifestations of HF uptake are examined as a discursive chain: uptake from advocacy genres into policy and research genres, uptake from research genres into legislation, and uptake from legislation back into advocacy and HF proposals and projects. The second generic entity of uptake is the list of homeless subpopulations which has become emblematic of the value of inclusivity and which plays a critical role in advocacy uptake of HF.

To summarize current theorizing of uptake and genre and to suggest possible contributions this study offers, the next section elaborates the conceptual framework sketched above, drawing together the key concepts of uptake and uptake enactment, context as genre ecology and genre system, genre memory as shallow or deep, and genre disruption and re-stabilization. This summary is followed by a description of the methodology, a findings and discussion section analyzing the discursive chain of HF uptake, and a conclusion.

2 Uptake, Genre Memory, and Genre Stability

Uptake as Translation Across Boundaries

Within a rhetorical genre framework (Giltrow & Stein, 2009; Frow, 2006; Bazerman 1994; Miller, 1984), this study adopts the contextual constructs of "genre system" (Bazerman, 1994) and "genre ecology" (Spinuzzi and Zachry, 2000) to examine the genre-based concept of uptake (Devitt, 2009; Freadman, 1987, 2001, 2012) and its relation to genre memory. Genre is treated as a socio-cognitively shared blueprint for social action; uptake as a multi-directional, dialogical and strategic translation of a discursive event across genre boundaries (Freadman, 2002); and every genre instantiation as a unique discursive event that can be both unpredictable and generically recognizable. In retheorizing Austin's concept of uptake (1962/1975) as "translation," Freadman (1987/1994) describes uptake as always minimally "two-way" and not, as apparently with Austin, either "one-way" or "two-way" (1962/1975, p. 117): uptake is the "bi-directional relationship that holds between . . . a text and . . . its 'interpretant,'" which Freadman (2002) names "the uptake text" (p. 40). As Freadman proposes, uptake entails both expectation and strategy: "My text is . . . a move in a game. It expects an uptake" (1987/1994, p. 62). Uptake is therefore dialogical for it anticipates an audience's response and involves both "addressivity" (Bakhtin, 1986, p. 95) and strategic translation. As translation, uptake is an inter- or intrageneric "movement" (Freadman, 2002, p. 44) which can occur either more or less automatically as in routine institutional boundary crossings along well-worn discursive paths (for example, medical and police reports crossing into insurance genres), or strategically by a dominant force (for example, the promotion of corporate priorities in government policy), or tactically from less powerful forces or groups into a dominant institution (for example the adoption of Indigenous healing practices into medicine). In all cases, uptake can have unexpected effects, particularly when different factions within a genre ecology jointly mediate the boundaries of a genre or genre system's history. In her analysis of a sequence of strategic uptakes that translated a legal death "sentence" from one jurisdiction into another jurisdiction where it became an "execution," Freadman (2002) shows the phenomenon of translation across jurisdictions and argues for a conceptual relationship between genre and uptake: "when uptake crosses the boundary between ceremonies, and *a fortiori* between jurisdictions, it mediates between genres" (p. 44). She argues that "genre theory can tell us something important about the quotation of generic forms outside their standard jurisdictional frames" (p. 46), and she implies (2012) that uptake needs the concepts of generic boundaries and of the generic frame to be meaningfully analyzed. She resists expanding this theoretical frame, and argues that "[w]e cannot ... reflect productively on uptake outside of discussions of genre, nor is it productive to theorize the action of genres without uptake" (p. 560). Genre boundaries, of course, are not always clearly discernible for there is much latitude for overlapping of genres, for embedding, hybridizing, and mixing of genres. However, for the purposes of this study, boundaries are approached from the perspective of activity within genre which constitutes the gravitational pull of what Bakhtin (1981) calls a genre's "sphere of activity": a "social language . . . peculiar to a specific stratum of society ... within a given social system at a given time" (Holquist & Emerson, 1981, p. 430, paraphrasing Bakhtin). Miller's definition of genre similarly implies boundaries that frame a "fusion" and "constellation": a genre is "a constellation of recognizable forms bound together by an internal dynamic" that "fuses" recurrent "substantive, stylistic, and situational characteristics" (Miller, 1984, p. 152)

Since uptake implicates more than one genre, there has been a move in theory and research from analyzing single or paired genres toward a consideration of how multiple genres interact. This movement has led theorists to posit concepts such as an "evolving generic array" (Freadman, 1999), "genre set" (Devitt, 1991), "genre assemblages" (Spinuzzi, 2003), "genre suite" (Berkenkotter and Hanganu-Bresch, 2011), and the additional network concepts of "genre system" (Bazerman, 1994) and "genre ecology" (Spinuzzi & Zachry, 2000). While each of these has some explanatory power for our understanding of uptake and genre, this study utilizes Spinuzzi and Zachry's concept of a "genre ecology" (2000) and Bazerman's concept of "genre system," which seem to be the most compatible constructs for optimizing the explanatory power of a genre analysis of uptake enactments.

GENRE MEMORY AND BOUNDARY-CROSSING

A central concept in the present study of HF uptake is genre memory. To develop genre memory as a productive analytical concept in relation to uptake, I have followed Tachinos's (2016) adoption of Spinuzzi and Zachry's conceptual framework of a network of multiple genres, a "genre ecology," to situate the play of uptake: a network is made up "an inter-related group of genres (artifact types and interpretive habits that have developed around them) used to jointly mediate the activities that allow people to accomplish complex objectives" (p. 172). The network contains several generic threads that "are connected through contingency" (p. 173); they are drawn together in uptake enactments, in unpredictable ways, each thread with its attendant and different "genre residue" or memory. Within a sphere of activity or genre system, like advocacy, over time the network of practices and genres—the genre ecology—develops a collective social memory of genre activity, what Spinuzzi (2003) refers to as its "genre residue." The analyses of uptake here focus on genre activity as moments of uptake enactments and the process that leads to the effects of uptake, whether non-problematic, disruptive, or constructive. These generic threads derive from both "official" and "unofficial" genres, "central" and "peripheral" genres (p. 176). This study of HF uptake adds this hierarchical, parallel metaphor of "high" and "low" level genres (Frow, 2006) from genre system theory. It is suggested that each generic thread derived from a genre ecology is tied to a specific "sphere of activity" —for example, advocacy or research—with an intra-generic but open system of related genres that function as tools for participants in that sphere.

Genre memory, then, accompanies uptake from one genre and its sphere of activity and affects how it is received in another genre, that is, in the uptake text, just as the receiving genre recontextualizes genre memory. Freadman marshals Bakhtin's insight (1963) that "a genre lives in the present, but always *remembers* its past, its beginning" (Bakhtin, 1963, p. 106). As Morson and Emerson explain, genre bears both the past and present as a kind of "double-voicedness" (Bakhtin, 1986, pp. 110-119):

> Because genres are so often adapted from previous genres, they may carry the potential to resume their past usage and so to redefine a present experience in an additional way. . . . Genres shaped in one area of life may be imported into another. (Morson and Emerson, p. 293).

As each instance of uptake inhabits a new context, it also arrives impressed with its past. For example, uptake of HF from research by the federal government involves the negotiation of research findings with government's practices of fiscal restraint and historical underfunding for marginal groups. Similarly, uptake of the government's model for HF by service providers involves the negotiation with past practices and values of care of homeless people and the way government funding has traditionally been secured and used to help homeless people. Freadman (2002) pursues the relationship between genre memory and uptake and extends Bakhtin's insight about this relationship: "uptakes ... have memories—long, ramified, intertextual and intergeneric memories" (p. 40). As noted, in the context of power relations, rhetorical strategy can transform uptake offered by one genre so that it may be translated, "brokered," or even repurposed (Dryer, 2012; Tachino, 2012; Bawarshi, 2012). This alteration can be a routine or a subversive translation, for "the uptake text has the power not to so confirm this [prior] generic status, which it may modify minimally, or even utterly by taking its object as some other kind" (p. 40). In cases where the uptake text may repurpose another generic entity, conforming to a new generic context can appear to be an infelicitous version of uptake to those participants who have a different memory rooted in their genre system.

Also building on Bakhtin's concept of "genre memory," Spinuzzi (2003) suggests that "genre residue" is constitutive of genre as "a sort of social memory" (p. 43) that "represents [a] community's history of problem-solving" (p. 48). Spinuzzi (2003) adopts the notion of genre memory in his analysis of the multiple genres and systems involved in information design applications to analyze the social memory of a genre's problem-solving history. He summarizes and incorporates Morson and Emerson's commentary (1990) on Bakhtin's theory of genre and memory: genres, he suggests—and more widely, the interactions that hold together a genre system—carry the memory of not only propositions, but also certain dispositions of genre'd positions and value (Spinuzzi, 2003). Genre memory conditions future uptake: "Genres are the residue of past behaviour, an accretion that shapes, guides, and constrains future behaviour" (Spinuzzi, 1990, p. 290). These genre "residues" become particularly salient for certain genre participants in situations of unexpected uptake and can become reified objects of contention and struggle—especially where uptake crosses generic boundaries in contexts of asymmetrical power relations and brings into focus the evidence of power in both its conspicuous presences and its "notable absences" (Devitt, 2009, p. 34). In this monograph, the detection of a "notable absence" and participants' consequent resistance to or criticism of uptake with such notable absences, are analyzed, in part, by drawing a distinction between deep "ramified," active genre memory and shallow, fossilized or abbreviated genre memory. It seems that, where uptake reflects shallow memory of key genre content, those participants in a genre system's sphere of activity who have a more robust shared history of the beliefs, practices, and values of activity are likely to object to the omission, and, in turn, begin to re-translate uptake according to their remembered and reiterated values.

Genre Contingency and Stability

In his analysis of uptake from experts and research into the public inquiry genre, Tachino (2016) suggests supplanting Freadman's "bi-directional" model of uptake (from her tennis metaphor), with a multi-directional model of uptake composed of "multiple" generic threads and "connections," as in a game of "multiple tennis shots." He proposes that each "shot" or activated connection involves the motivations and influences of an "intertextual thread" (p. 182). In adapting Spinuzzi and Zachry's concept of "genre ecology" (2000), he explains how a genre ecology can illuminate this network of connections, its multiple generic affordances, and uptake selections. In particular, the openness of this network can account for the contingency and unpredictability of the effects of uptake enactments.

The dynamics of uptake as strategic improvisation and its potential for disruption and de-stabilization have been the subject of a series of studies by Freadman (1987/1994, 2002, 2012). Traditional genre analysis, however, has tended to treat genre as a more-or-less stable phenomenon, and this stability is certainly a necessary, temporary condition for corpus-based analysis. However, this methodological requirement—to hold an object of analysis in place for close examination—can lead to a tendency to assume an inherent stability in genre. This assumption, however, has been challenged by scholars interested in rhetorical agency who emphasize the improvisational nature of genre performance and the "stabilized for now" status of genre integrity (Schryer, 1993, p. 208).

Just as contingency can make for unpredictable uptake and desta-bilize an uptake text, the recontextualization in a new generic context can reconfigure and reorganize the uptake genre so that it paradoxically becomes "restabilized-for-now." As Freadman (2002) has asserted, what has been taken up confirms its new generic existence by "conforming itself to" the genre of the receiving text (p. 40). This conformity to a new genre becomes a temporary stabilizing force through the co-occurrence of change and accommodation. Sometimes this is seen by participants as a fitting rhetorical response to a discursive event (e.g., when partici-pants perceive the rhetorical exigence has been felicitously addressed: the receiving genre apparently unproblematically—automatically?—accom-modates the uptake). At other times participants experience the insertion of uptake into a new genre and context as a kind of "hostile takeover" by what Bhatia (2004) calls a colonizing genre—in his example, when advertising colonizes research genres (p. 58). In extreme takeovers, the receiving genre "utterly" transforms the uptake text (Freadman, 2002, p. 40), in which case, subsequent uptake may be subject to tactical resis-tance and creative interpretation.

Regardless of how disruptive uptake may be, the destabilizing mo-ment is relatively "fleeting": "genre uptakes reveal themselves in fleet-ing moments of alignment with, or disruption of, writers' 'complex and sometimes conflicting templates of … discourses, … visions of life, and notions, … relations with others and the world'" (Lu, 2004, p. 28 cited by Dryer, 2016, p. 61). After such a discursive event, genre seems to re-organize itself as a more-or-less changed socio-cognitive phenomenon, reconfigured around uptake from another genre but also as a recogniz-able social action and viable "form of life" within its own genre system. What has disturbed and perhaps altered the centripetal forces that make a genre's context and form coherent (its internal dynamic fusion of form, content, and situation) realigns, absorbs, contains, or ejects part or all of the proffered uptake. In this way genre "holds" social and power rela-tions together (Bawarshi, 2016b, pp. 52, 57) "in an 'alternative' but rec-ognizable form and situation."

It seems that uptake simultaneously both frees itself from one genre and encounters the boundary of another. One might say that uptake de-pends on genre for its dialogical freedom, and genre, as an ecology or as a system, accommodates and enables the "game" to continue within and across its spheres of activity.

The following analyses trace the trajectories of "uptake artifacts" or "texts that respond to other texts" (Dryer, 2012), both textually and contextually as "genre residue" or memory—that which adheres to resituated language in its recontextualized texts. To some extent, genre memory and the contingencies of uptake are shown to account for the differences in dynamics and effects in key types of uptake, which can be characterized as unproblematic, disruptive, and constructive HF uptakes. In the case of non-problematic uptake, a social issue may be moved towards progressive change (uptake of HF from advocacy into local policy and then research); in the case of disruptive uptake (uptake of HF from governance into advocacy and the service-provider sphere), social agendas may be derailed when a "notable absence" disorients participants' expectations, that is, when uptake crosses genre boundaries and comes to exist in what Freadman (1987/1994) calls different "ceremonies," "tak[ing] with them the signs of the lost ceremony, connoting that ceremony and the social relations it governs" (1994, p. 61). And in the case of reconstructive uptake (tactical uptake of HF from governance into advocacy and social action) a creative, collaborative response to disorientation that "remembers" a genre's history may constitute a kind of compensation.

3 Methodology: Ethnography and Discourse Analysis

The methodology for this study is qualitative and ethnographic, involving both textual analysis (key genres and texts) and contextual analysis (meetings and interviews), with some quantitative analysis of two written genres. In the context of the increasing number of homeless people in the Lower Mainland of BC, a crescendo of voices about the "homeless problem," and a strong interest in the struggle for the homeless, I began this study as a search for the presence of homeless people and their housing in municipal discourse, first doing a genre analysis of Official Community Plans. At that level of official discourse, my analysis showed homeless people to be next to invisible. Curious about this lacuna in municipalities that were clearly grappling with homelessness, I turned to the level of advocacy then, analyzing several texts, including municipal Housing and Homelessness Strategic Plans (HSPs), and key relevant contexts, most notably the monthly meetings of two task forces on housing and homelessness. A central focus among advocates has been the Housing First approach to homelessness, which ultimately became the object of my research—that is, the process and instantiation of HF uptake from its early emergence in the U.S. to its implementation in Canada. The goal has been to elucidate the role of genre, uptake, and memory in the struggle for this marginalized group, to use the phenomenon of HF as a way of examining both the contestation and cooperation between advocacy and more powerful groups, primarily government, but also its alignments with the media and certain publics.

Genre memory exists in both textual and contextual dimensions, and both can be traced historically, in textual and in oral form. Following Freadman (2012), both dimensions of uptake are treated as "a sequence of events in time and across a variety of temporal sequences" such that any analysis of uptake "goes back as far as we find it useful to take it (hence the memory of discursive events)" (p. 558). Analyses here follow the uptake of two "forms" and their "in-forming" contexts from advocacy genres into policy, research and governance genres, specifically 1) the recurrent categories of homeless and "at-risk" populations, and 2) the discursive forms of HF models and definitions. Key textual sources examined include advocacy policies and bulletins, municipal homelessness strategic plans, official community plans, federal funding guideline documents, research articles, government press releases, and media reports. To contextualize the textual analyses, and to provide evidence of uptake of these discursive entities in the oral discourse of participants in the homelessness genre system, the author developed a participant-observer relationship over three years (2011-2014) with two local advocacy communities through attendance at a series of monthly meetings of two municipally-embedded homelessness and housing task forces, a small number of bi-monthly meetings of a homeless foundation board, and one meeting of a local outreach worker network (all were taped and key excerpts transcribed). Data also includes notes from observations at a 2014 meeting of the Metro-Vancouver Regional Steering Committee on Homelessness, of which the author was then a "general" member[1].

In addition, data was drawn from 21 taped and transcribed interviews (2011-2016) with various stakeholders, including service providers, city planners, task force chairs, city councillors, outreach workers, a Chez Soi researcher, and member of the Metro-Vancouver Regional Steering Committee on Homelessness (RSCH). (See Table 1.) Interviews ranged from 45 to 90 minutes and were semi-structured with wide latitude for unsolicited commentary. Common topics were stakeholders' roles, values and histories in the homelessness system, their understandings of HF, their knowledge of funding sources, their strategies for funding eligibility and service provision, and their reasons for persisting in their roles or for stepping back or resigning.

---

1. The Metro-Vancouver Regional Steering Committee on Homelessness has three types of membership: Constituency Table (agency members only who decide on policies and actions) Advisory Groups (individual and agency members who recommend policies and actions), and General Membership (individual and agency members who exchange information and are invited to events). (from "Become a RSCH Member," RSCH website)

Table 1: Stakeholder Interviews 2011- 2016

Stakeholder	Number of Participants	Number of Interviews
Service-Providers	6	6
City Planners	3	3
Task Force Chairs	2	4 (2 each)
City Councillors	2	5 (3 and 2)
Outreach Workers	2	1 (joint)
Chez Soi Researcher	1	1
RSCH Constituent Member and Former Chair	1	3

These meetings and interviews provide discursive evidence of uptake and context (social, political, economic) for interpreting textual uptake selections, motivations, and responses. The transcript analyses involved coding for key themes as they emerged: values such as inclusivity and the right to housing, historical understandings of the HF approach and responses to the federal HF model, and community practices such as collaboration and improvisation.

Textual analyses of relevant documents trace two textual chains as they cross from advocacy genres into municipal homelessness strategic plans, research initiatives and reports, and then into legislation and implementation: 1) the development of categories of homeless and "at-risk" populations and 2) HF uptake.

A preliminary examination of 14 BC Official Community Plans (OCPs), a municipal governance genre, used Ant Conc software to count mentions of "homeless/ness" and "shelters" as indices of homeless (in)visibility and government and community priorities on homelessness. The results, which showed a virtual absence of "homeless" people in OCPs, motivated a subsequent analysis of 10 BC Housing and Homelessness Strategic Plans (HSPs): 1) to trace how the precursor term for "HF," "permanent housing," came to compete with and supplant the previously dominant model for homelessness funding (the continuum of care involving services and "temporary shelters"), and 2) to identify those homeless population categories cited by homelessness task force members at the municipal level as needing services and housing. This comprehensive list of homeless categories became emblematic of the advocacy community's ethic of inclusiveness which has informed how they practice advocacy and care, and which strongly influenced how they negotiated the federal government's HF model and funding criteria. A list of categories of homeless populations was compiled by manually tag-ging every subpopulation mentioned in the HSPs. It was reduced to 21 clusters of key terms. For example, the "mentally ill" category subsumes mentions of "mentally ill, mental health, and SAMI (severe addictions and/or mental illness"). The key terms were then used as the basis for ANT Concordance Digital corpus software (Ant Conc) analyses of the HSPs to identify: a) how many HSPs included each homeless category, and b) the frequency of mention overall for each category. (See Table 2.)

Table 2. Homeless Population Categories: Key Words

Aboriginal
absolutely homeless
abuse, victims of violence, domestic violence
addiction
correction system, leaving institutions, discharged
couch-surfing
disability, cannot live independently
extremely dysfunctional, people in crisis
eviction
families
hard-to-house, hardest to serve
HIV/AIDS, hep
injection drug users, IV users, methadone client
low income, poor, disadvantaged, living in poverty, in need and spending at least their
    income on shelter, income/shelter assistance, core housing need, precariously
    housed, high-risk, low paying jobs
mentally ill, mental health, SAMI (severe addictions and/or mental illness)
seniors, elderly
sex industry/worker
skill development, lacking education and skills, marketable skills
street homeless/campers/population, on the street, in shelters, city's streets, living on
    the street, sleeping bodies, doorways
women
youth

These preliminary analyses (2010-2012) provided a basis and direc-tion for the key follow-up research (2012-2016) that traces the uptake of the HF model from advocacy genres like HSPs and task force meetings into policy and research, from research into federal legislation in the form of the government's 2013 budget, and then from government back into advocacy and HF implementation. Following Emmons' approach to analysis of uptake, I have examined texts to track the HF "textual chain," "marking and referring to the textual traces of the process" (2009, 134-140) as it crosses texts and genres. This involved examining references to both the HF model and its predecessor, the traditional continuum-of-care treatment-first model. Ethics approval for the project was received from the Research Ethics Board of Douglas College (New Westminster, BC) and all participants provided informed consent.

4 The Discursive Chain of HF Uptake: Advocacy, Policy, Research, Governance, Advocacy

Within the homelessness genre system there has evolved a consensus endorsing the HF "solution to homelessness," from its early proposals by advocates in both the US and Canada (1990s) to its eventual adoption by the Canadian federal government (2013) and service-provider implementation (2014-2016). This developing consensus has involved a series of uptakes, each retranslating HF. Where the translation of HF has reflected advocates' core values and goals, as in municipal ten-year strategic plans to end homelessness, uptake has been more-or-less unproblematic. However, the retranslation of HF into legislation posed challenges and problems for advocates and service-providers who had worked for decades under the traditional continuum of care focused on services and treatment. The shift to the HF model and its funding priorities disrupted these practices, an apparently unintended effect of the federal government's move to HF. As will be argued, these genre participants had a deeper experience and shared memory of the homelessness genre system than that of the federal government whose HF funding criteria was motivated by the institutional "memory" of its own political and economic genre systems. The government's endorsement of HF came primarily because of the Chez Soi research results and a proactive Senator who promoted HF, but also involved collaboration with advocacy groups. Following the Chez Soi approach, government funding targeted only certain homeless populations, and it did not provide the requisite funding for health services and rental subsidies that had been crucial in the success of Chez Soi. Moreover, the bulk of the funding would now go to HF projects and HF readiness instead of the services and supports that traditionally had been funded.

The findings are presented in five sections, tracing the uptake pathways and discursive chain of both the HF model and the categories of homeless populations identified in advocacy:

1. Uptake of HF from Advocacy into Policy (HSPs)
2. Uptake of Categories of Homeless and At-Risk Populations from Advocacy into Policy (HSPs)
3. Uptake of HF from Advocacy into Research
4. Uptake of HF from Advocacy and Research into Governance (Legislation)
5. Uptake of HF from Governance into Advocacy and Service-Provision

The first two sub-sections examine the early and relatively slower stage of uptake of the HF model and the categories of homeless populations from advocacy, which proceeded as two concurrent discursive chains from advocacy into HSPs, and from advocacy into research genres. As municipalities were incorporating the HF approach and developing categories of homeless populations eligible for government help, early research began to study the effectiveness of HF sites and projects. The last three sub-sections follow the more recent and significant uptakes by government-funded research and government policy.

UPTAKE OF HF FROM ADVOCACY INTO POLICY (HSPs)

In the 1990s and 2000s, the HSP genre emerged at the local, municipal level in Canada as an adaptation of both the generic institutional strategic plan, a governance and corporate genre, and the prior American "10 year plan to end homelessness" which had originated through advocacy groups and local task forces in cities, primarily in the U.S., in the 1990s. In this genre merger, governance discourses came into contact with human rights and social justice discourses.

In the wake of these American ten-year plans, municipalities began to strike joint task forces of advocates, service-providers, social planners, and politicians to collaboratively develop HSPs which were subsequently endorsed by city councils. The dynamics of homelessness advocacy have played out over the last few decades as a tension in HSPs between a "housing-first" approach (often expressed in its earlier formulation as "permanent" housing) as uptake from advocacy policies targeting the chronically and episodically homeless, and the traditional "continuum of care" model that emphasized providing services and treatment and temporary "shelters," as opposed to "supported" and "independent" housing," for homeless people (e.g., see Figure 1). "Shelters" are, by definition, temporary housing and are usually listed at one end of the housing and care spectrum, with affordable permanent housing at the other end.

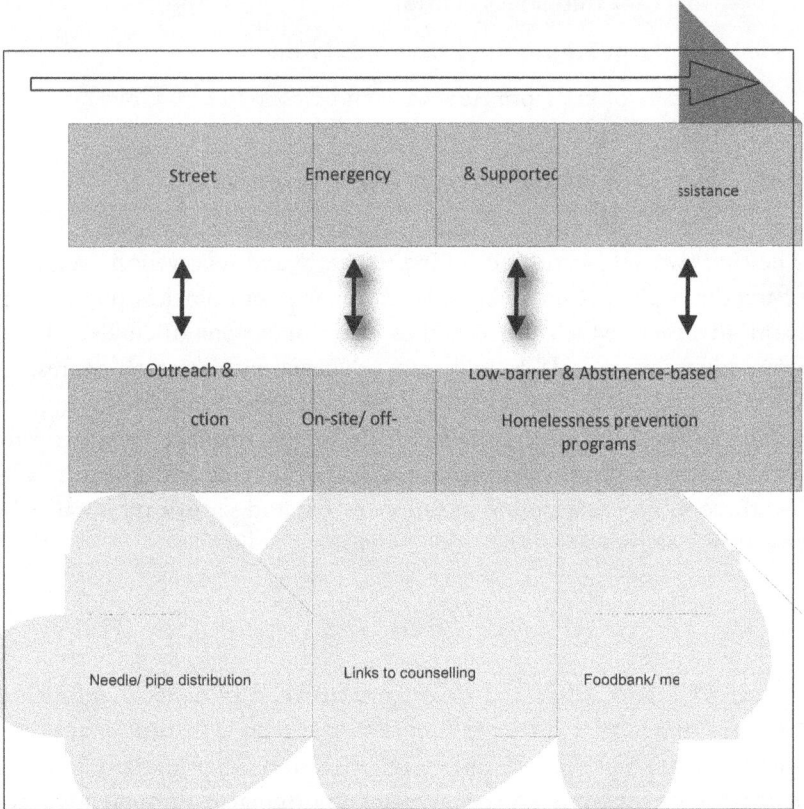

Figure 1: Housing and Support Services Continuum (*Nanaimo's Response to Homelessness Action Plan*, 2008).

The continuum of housing and care services was adopted in BC in 1999/2000 when the province began to provide funding for supportive housing and assisted living for seniors based on and correlated with a continuum of housing and health care services. Later, when homelessness became part of the province's housing agenda, it began including shelters for homeless people in the continuum (email correspondence, consultant, May 14/12). Some HSPs still cite, verbatim, explicit uptake of the continuum from the provincial plan, *Housing Matters BC* (2006), which frames its overall strategy based on the continuum of housing:

> In developing this strategy, government looked at the continuum of housing need from homelessness to the need for affordable rental housing and homeownership. . . . While this strategy addresses the full housing continuum, a primary focus is ensuring B.C.'s most vulnerable citizens and those with low incomes have improved access to housing assistance. (*Housing Matters BC,* 2006, pp. 2-3)

In a preliminary analysis of 10 HSPs, eight were found to include a version of the concept of the "continuum" or "spectrum" of housing and care, defined as a model that uses "income as the determining factor of the form of housing needed" (*Kelowna Housing Strategy,* 2012, 8) and that aims to move homeless people from addiction to recovery and then into housing. Six gave priority to either "permanent" housing or a "housing first" approach over the continuum model; four promoted the continuum model as the priority. This finding illustrates the shift that was beginning to take place in HSPs away from the continuum of housing and care framework to a "housing first" approach, with "permanent housing" the preferred option over temporary housing and support services which, advocates argued, simply perpetuates the cycle of homelessness, institutionalizing homelessness instead of ending it. Since the 1990s, policy makers, researchers and advocates have adopted the term "Housing-First" from its original association with "Pathways to Housing" (New York) and "Beyond Shelter" (Los Angeles). "The Pathways" (PHF) approach has been popularized by its founder and advocate, Sam Tsemberis (Gaetz, Scott, & Gulliver, 2013, p. 3). Uptake in Canada has come primarily from HF initiatives in American cities such as New York, Portland, and Minneapolis, and in Canada from Toronto and Calgary.

Explicit evidence of the shift in advocacy to an emphasis on the HF approach is found in policy papers by advocacy organizations such as the Canadian Alliance to End Homelessness (CAEH, 2000), the Federation of Canadian Municipalities (FCM, 2008), and the Union of BC Municipalities (UBCM, 2008). The CAEH derived its plan and emphasis on HF directly from its American counterpart, the NAEH:

> *A Plan, Not a Dream* is directly derived from a document of the same name developed by the National Alliance to End Homelessness (NAEH) in the United States. (*A Plan, Not a Dream:*

How to End Homelessness in 10 years, NAEH, 2000, p. 3). . . .
Core to effective community plans is the concept of Housing
First. . . . A successful and transformational housing model used
in a number of Canadian and American communities. (*A Plan,
Not a Dream,* CAEH, 2000).

The FCM alludes to the "recent" emergence of HF, for which it provides
a definition, "supportive housing as a first step":

> In updating their community plans, most communities have
> emphasized the need to move beyond managing homelessness
> to ending it. . . . The term "housing first" has recently emerged
> and places priority on providing supportive housing as a first
> step out of homelessness and a key to preventing homelessness.
> (*Sustaining the Momentum: Recommendations for a National Ac-
> tion Plan on Housing and Homelessness,* FCM, Jan. 2008, p. 12)

The UBCM refers to the apparent evidence in the U.S. of the positive
effects of HF:

> Federal officials in the United States have attributed much
> of the decline [in homelessness between 2005 and 2007] to
> the "housing first" strategy that has been adopted across the
> country . . . there appears to be a consensus emerging that an
> integrated approach is needed to effectively address the home-
> lessness problem: "Home first" approach. . . . (*Policy Paper #2,
> Affordable Housing and Homelessness Strategy,* UBCM, Sept. 24,
> 2008, p. 2).

The shift in Canadian social policy away from a strictly "services" and
temporary "shelter" approach to a HF approach has been the recent cul-
mination of at least 30 years of ten year plans to end homelessness that
either implicitly or explicitly promote a HF approach. As uptake from
advocacy and policy endorsements, several BC municipalities have incorporated the "housing-first" approach in HSPs, for example:

> . . . services should be provided to people in permanent housing,
> not in the homeless system. This notion is commonly referred
> to as 'Housing First' (*City of Kelowna: Mayor's Task Force to End
> Homelessness,* 2007, p. 9).

Like those in most other cities, the Kamloops Homelessness Action Plan takes a *'Housing First' approach* to homelessness. This means that establishing a home is top priority; nothing else can take root unless there is a roof over one's head. (City of Kamloops, 2011, p. 25, Italics in original.)

Using the *housing first* approach, homeless individuals are moved directly, and as quickly as possible, into permanent housing . . . . (*Homelessness Action Strategy and Implementation Plan for New Westminster*, 2006, p. 4, Italics in original).

Many cities in the U.S. and Canada now have HSPs modelled on American "ten year plans to end homelessness," of which a primary principle is the HF approach. Policy analysis by advocacy organizations and academics confirm this shift:

Housing First is a successful and transformational housing model used in a number of Canadian and American communities and is at the heart of all successful 10 Year Plans to End Homelessness. (NAEH website, 2013)

This shift . . . to a priority placed on housing without treatment expectations . . . labeled housing-first (HF) . . . has rapidly acquired wide-spread adoption by communities with 10-year plans to end homelessness in Canada and the U.S. (e.g., Calgary, Toronto, Minneapolis, San Diego, New York) (Waegemakers, Schiff, & Rook, 2012, p.4)

For over a decade now, submitting a ten-year plan has been a requirement of Canadian applications for federal funding for homelessness.

Significantly, however, even if HF is cast as a priority, all ten HSPs retain the continuum of housing and care as part of their policy framework, an orientation to the federal government's conventional funding criteria targeting services and shelters for, not only the chronically homeless, but also at-risk populations. This conventional homelessness funding criteria is still a funding category in the federal budget, but since the federal adoption of HF in 2013 it has been greatly reduced, with most funds designated for HF. Until February 2013, legislated eligibility criteria for federal homelessness funds show the dominance of the continuum framework ("a seamless continuum of supports and services" [*Housing Partnership Strategy*, Government of Canada, 2011]) with no reference to permanent housing for the homeless. For example, the Homelessness Partnering Strategy (pre-2013 budget) cites, as funding "priorities . . . for the Metro Vancouver region," the usual support services (transitional and supportive housing, emergency shelter services, mental health and addiction services, outreach services, etc.) and the traditional categories of homeless and at-risk populations (those with addictions, the mentally ill, aboriginals, families, youth, seniors, women, official language minorities) (Homelessness Partnership Strategy, *Terms and Strategies,* 2011).

Prior to 2013, the co-existence of both the continuum of services and housing and the HF approach resulted in a certain ambivalence in HSPs and in provincial policy, which can be seen as indicative of a "transformation" in process in the struggle for the homeless, what Holland and Lave (2001) have characterized as the local expression of a general "enduring struggle"— "a two-way generative traffic that . . . capture[s] local struggles and . . . cultural practices *as they are undergoing transformation"* (p. 22, Italics in original). The orientations towards both traditional prior federal budget criteria and advocacy for a "housing first" approach appear in both advocacy and government genres. For example, the 2007 BC provincial housing strategy gestures towards a "housing first" approach—"The emphasis shifts from . . . temporary shelter beds to helping people break out of the cycle of poverty" (*Housing Matters BC, BC Housing,* p. 6)—but also refers explicitly to "the full housing continuum" (p. 1). For the Union of BC Municipalities, who endorses the housing first approach, such apparent ambivalence was disconcerting in terms of funding uncertainty:

> It is not clear whether or not the province has adopted a housing first strategy to address homelessness or is adopting some other policy. (Union of BC Municipalities, *Policy Paper #2,* 2008, 5).

Pre-2013, the co-existence of these orientations was also present at the regional level of Metro-Vancouver, whose ten-year plan did not refer to the HF model, yet whose actual practice was to support HF initiatives. Until 2014, Metro-Vancouver's Regional Steering Committee on Homelessness's ten-year HSP eschewed any reference to or suggestion of "housing first" (*3 Ways to Home: The Regional Homelessness Plan for Greater Vancouver, Summary,* 2005, 2), yet a former chair of the Steering Committee reports that in their adjudications of Homelessness Partnership Strategy funding applications, "Metro-Van does have a housing-first principle" and "probably what the [provincial] Ministry would say is their fundamental principle is that it's a housing-first model" (Interview, May 19/12). Pre-2013, all funding criteria were oriented to "services" for traditional "populations at-risk" in the context of the continuum of housing and care. As noted, early implementations of the housing-first approach, which municipalities advocated and worked toward, were more salient in practice than in the textual dimension of the genre, an example of the phenomenon that textual change typically lags behind contextual or social change. It wasn't until 2014 that Metro-Vancouver, as a response to the 2013 federal budget criteria, undertook a revision of its HSP expressly to focus on HF priorities. Notably, the 2014 revision of the provincial government's policy, *Housing Matters BC*, makes no mention of the continuum of housing.

As research in the U.S. and EU accumulated evidence of the ineffectiveness of the continuum of care (or "staircase services") approach, policy analysts reported these negative evaluations and recommended replacing it with an HF approach:

> The Continuum of Care programme [in the US] had some success, but evaluations of these staircase services also showed that many chronically homeless people were not being resettled (Sosin et al., 1995; Orwin et al., 1999; Hoch, 2000). Service users were becoming stuck on particular steps, being evicted or abandoning services because of strict rules. EU research on staircase services for homeless people also began reporting similar findings (Sahlin, 2005; Busch-Geertsema and Sahlin, 2007; Atherton and McNaughton-Nicholls, 2008). (Pleace, 2011, p. 116)

When studies began to show the effectiveness of HF over the conventional services model, governments in North America and Europe embraced HF, largely for its cost-effectiveness. Advocates and policy-makers came to contrast HF to "the standard approach to working with homeless people . . . characterized as a 'treatment-first' or 'treatment as usual' approach," whereby people who are homeless are placed in emergency and other services and then non-HF supported living environments (such as transitional housing) until they are deemed 'ready' for independent living" (Gaetz, Scott, and Gulliver, 2013, p. 2). Unlike HF, 'treatment-first' models are more regulated and compliance-based.

Uptake of Categories of Homeless and At-Risk Populations from Advocacy into Policy (HSPs)

In Canada, over the last three decades, advocates have developed an increasingly comprehensive list of homeless and at-risk populations who they cite as deserving of government support. These key sub-groups have emerged from advocacy, outreach research and media representations of homeless people. Studies of media representations indicate two dominant types: 1) those who are homeless as a result of structural causes who are represented as deserving of community or government support (typically, single mothers, youth, seniors, the mentally ill, and drug addicted), and 2) those who are homeless as a result of individuals' poor choices who are therefore represented as less deserving of government support (Schneider, Chamberlain, & Hodgetts, 2010). Homelessness advocates favour the structural causes explanation and cite numerous categories of homeless populations that should be eligible for support. This list of categories is inclusive of people who are at-risk of homelessness in contrast to the less inclusive, "street homeless" people in policy and research genres. Official government policies tend to cite the traditional list as those categories that governments deem eligible for specific kinds of social services funding and temporary shelter and tend to exclude other "at-risk" and "hidden homeless" categories such as the recently unemployed or evicted, recent immigrants in overcrowded housing, sex trade workers, or couch-surfing students. These other categories have, nevertheless, been taken up and cited in municipal advocacy genres, specifically in municipal HSPs.

This list of populations, as generic "form," is reiterated in all HSPs and tends to be inclusive of virtually everyone at potential risk of homelessness. Advocacy efforts are then focused on including more populations for homeless services in government policy. The expanded list is a key construction in the struggle for the homeless; in effect, it became part of the history, genre practice and memory, and deep consciousness of advocates. Believing housing is a human right, advocates came to associate HF with this expanded list of people at risk of homelessness. While the proliferation of categories of homeless populations may have been influenced initially by funding categories, by 2013 it had also come to reflect significant uptake of the key HF principle of inclusiveness which permeated advocacy genres. This inclusiveness has emerged as an off-shoot of human rights discourse in Canada whereby advocates now see housing as a human right: "everyone is deemed to be 'housing-ready'" (Gaetz, 2010, p. 23). As Johnsen and Teixiera (2010) observe, "Housing First separates treatment from housing, considering the former voluntary and the latter a fundamental need and human right" (p. 6). Significantly, Sam Tsemberis, founder of the Pathways HF approach, also endorses the rights approach. According to the Pathways website, "Dr. Sam founded Pathways to Housing in New York City in 1992 based on the belief that housing is a human right." The website also shows expanded services for PHF clients which include not only "mental health" and "addiction" but also "medical care, income, and education" (2017, pp. 1-2). The United Nations now also endorses housing as human right.

As noted earlier, an analysis of HSPs for homeless and at-risk of homelessness populations yielded 21 categories, extending from people with serious mental illness, people with addictions, women fleeing violence, and sex workers, to those leaving the correctional system, the unemployed, those facing eviction, those without a care card, and people who are beneficiaries of food banks. There was, of course, some overlap among categories, for example, people with addiction and sex workers, and the unemployed, poor and families. The greatest recurrences reflect the standard categories (people with addictions, families, the poor, people with mental illness, aboriginals, youth and women), but many more populate the genre, as shown in Table 3.

While change was occurring in the genre of HSPs, in contrast and not surprisingly, at the municipal level of the Official Community Plan, a higher-level genre with greater monetary repercussions, the homeless were conspicuously textually marginal (Notably, more recently sections on social housing and homelessness have been added to OCPs). An Ant Conc analysis of General or Official Community Plans (OCPs) between 1998 and 2013 shows textual representations of "the homeless" are absent or rare (Table 4). Following Huckin (2002), to surmount the challenge to discourse analysis of "identify[ing] something that is absent" (p. 353), a qualitative content analysis model was adopted to compile key words found in two relevant sections of 14 OCPs: Affordable Housing sections (required by the Local Government Act [LGA], BC) and Social Needs sections, where references to "the homeless" and "shelters (housing for the homeless) occur. Each instance of these sections was analyzed for which of these subtopics is included and excluded (Huckin, p. 356) with a focus on "notable absences" (Devitt, 2009). Huckin defines these "textual silences" as "the omission of some piece of information that is pertinent to the topic at hand" (p. 348) yet salient elsewhere in the discourse. OCPs are intended to be "visions" of cities and, having originated as "land plans," they still retain major sections on "development" and "housing." In all but two of the 14 OCPs analyzed, the dearth of references to the "homeless" and their "shelters" is in stark contrast to the proliferation of homeless and at-risk categories in HSPs:

Table 3. Categories of Homeless or At-Risk Populations Instantiated in 10 B.C. Housing and Homelessness Strategic Plans

Homeless Population Category	Out of 10 HSPs	Frequency of Mention
Aboriginal	5	62
absolutely homeless	2	6
abuse, victims of violence, domestic violence	7	28
addiction	9	110
correction system, leaving institutions, discharged	5	19
couch-surfing	2	2
disability, cannot live independently	5	11
extremely dysfunctional, people in crisis	2	3
eviction	2	4
families	9	91
hard-to-house, hardest to serve	2	2
HIV/AIDS, hep	2	4
injection drug users, IV users, methadone client	2	7
low income, poor, disadvantaged, living in poverty, in need and spending at least their income on shelter, income/shelter assistance, core housing need, precariously housed, high-risk, low paying jobs	8	84
mentally ill, mental health, SAMI (severe addictions and/or mental illness)	8	70
seniors, elderly	4	13
sex industry/worker	2	2
skill development, lacking education and skills, marketable skills	2	3
street homeless/campers/population, on the street, in shelters, city's streets, living on the street, sleeping bodies, doorways	4	13
women	7	50
youth	8	54

Table 4. Mentions of "Homeless/ness" and "Shelters" in 14 B.C. Official Community Plans

OCPs (in 2014)	Homeless/ness	Shelters
Abbotsford (2005, pp. 1-70)	0	0
Campbell River (2012)	2	3
Chilliwack (1998)	0	0
Coquitlam (2004)	0	0
Kamloops (2004, pp. 1-74)	4	4
New Westminster (2011)	20	3
North Peace (2009, pp. 1-26)	0	0
Pitt Meadows (2007)	0	0
Port Coquitlam (2013)	2	0
Port Moody (2011)	9	4
Surrey (2013)		0
Victoria (2012)	23	10
Whistler (2011)	1	1
White Rock (2008)	0	0

Only 8 out of 14 OCPs refer to "the homeless," and 6 out of 14 refer to "shelter(s)," this despite the intense focus on the homeless in city discourse where planners, advocates, and councillors produce and use a range of relevant genres directly addressing housing and homelessness, sometimes with references to the OCP. As Freadman (2001) explains, uptake from one genre to another involves taking an object "from a set of possibles" (p. 48); while there is an "opportunity" to include a discursive entity (Huckin, p. 360), it is not always acted on. Where the term "homeless" does occur, it tends to be given less textual prominence and is often located at the bottom of a discursive hierarchy of special needs, usually at the end of a list of social groups, for example:

> These [special needs groups] include persons with disabilities and those requiring emergency shelter, such as those "at risk," youth and the homeless. (Victoria OCP, 2009)

> Vulnerable groups, such as people with disabilities, youth-at-risk, and the homeless will benefit . . . (Abbotsford OCP, 2005)

In another OCP, the homeless are sequestered with other special needs groups within parentheses:

> Continue to strive to satisfy the changing requirements of a diverse community including its special needs residents (e.g., physically disabled, homeless, mentally handicapped, mentally ill, visually or hearing impaired). ("Housing," OCP, New Westminster, 1998)

In another they appear in a footnote defining "special needs housing":

> *Special needs housing includes short-term emergency shelters for the homeless, transition houses for those fleeing domestic violence, group homes for young offenders, SRO's, and second-stage and permanent self-contained accommodation. ("Affordable Housing Policy" section, Chilliwack OCP, 1998)

Contextual evidence from meetings, interviews, and other low level genres suggests that this blockage of uptake of the general category of "homeless" people in OCPs reflects the struggle between local and senior governments over funding responsibility for homelessness. For example, the Kamloops OCP (2004) states that "senior levels of government will continue to be the prime source of funding to address issues of homelessness and housing affordability" and explicitly excludes the City from this responsibility: "the City of Kamloops is not a housing provider or manager" ("Affordable Housing" section, Kamloops OCP, 2004). This strategic avoidance of funding responsibility is coded textually as a reduction and marginalization of homeless people at the institutional level. Municipal leaders have repeatedly asserted that homelessness funding is a federal responsibility, and have called for increased federal funding, which local governments and task forces see as seriously inadequate. This has been the status quo for decades, with little indication of policy change at the federal level. While homelessness has arrived as a recognized social reality, with copious professional, social and municipal commentary, and while addressing it is enabled under "affordable housing,' at the foundational level of the OCP as a governance genre, there has been minimal textual uptake. According to Freadman, "it is at points such as these, where real power over outcomes is at stake" that there can be "the silencing" of less powerful genres "through the violence of translation" into a more powerful genre, "confirming the disempowerment of one jurisdiction and the power of the other" (pp. 44-47). A significant motivation for this "silence" in OCPs is the political stance adopted by municipalities and provinces in Canada that funding and solutions to homelessness are the responsibility of the federal government. Municipalities may thus seem ambivalent in their role as agents of change, as they protect the status quo (Herndl and Licona, 2007) in high-level genres, yet have elaborate strategic plans that actively take up the homelessness agenda at the local level.

UPTAKE OF HF FROM ADVOCACY INTO RESEARCH

Unanticipated developments at other sites in the homelessness genre system, however, have enabled uptake of HF, specifically PHF for mentally ill people who are homeless, into higher more powerful genres than HSPs. As Frow (2006) notes, "[g]enre systems form a shifting hierarchy, made up of tensions between 'higher' and 'lower' genres" (p. 71). Some genre systems are more conducive to hierarchical shifts: as Bazerman observes in his study of the legal genre system, which is rigorously hierarchical and affords only certain pathways for uptake, "[i]n domains [of genre systems] structured more loosely than the law, the sequencing and consequences of actions may be harder to discern, therefore allowing a wider array of consequent actions" (98). The relatively loose structuring of the homelessness genre system, which reaches local communities across the country and into three levels of government, affords a variety of resources and kairotic moments for uptake. One of these affordances came through the Mental Health Commission of Canada (MHCC), which was created in 2007 because of several serendipitous initiatives by a well net-worked Senator. The MHCC, which straddles both advocacy and research genre systems, was mandated to address the needs of chronically and episodically homeless people who have a mental illness or a dual diagnosis (mental illness and addiction). In their study of how the resulting pilot HF AH/CS project came about, MacNaughton et al. (2013) describe a series of events that led to the uptake of HF from advocacy and policy into government-sponsored research: what paved the way for the MHCC and the At Home/Chez Soi was a series of research-related uptakes by influential people and decision-makers in "response to the policy failure of community mental health in North America" (MacNaughton et al., 2013, p. 101).

A senate consultation led by Senator Michael Kirby produced the report *Out of the Shadows* (2006) which recommended "developing evidence-based, recovery-oriented supports for people with serious mental illness" and the creation of a Commission (p. 101). Kirby became Chair of the Commission. At the same time (2008) he was asked by a "senior member of the Canadian government" to help develop a "project for homeless people with mental illness in Vancouver" (p. 103). In his consultations with researchers, the project grew to five cities. The impetus for these developments was two-fold. The first was negative reporting in both the national and international media on the City of Vancouver's treatment of homeless people as it prepared for the 2010 Olympics. The City was severely criticized by a "housing Czar" from the US, a report from the United Nations, and an Olympic watchdog coalition, prompting the mayor of Vancouver to remind the federal government that "the world will be arriving at our doorsteps" (p. 103). The second development was a consensus that homelessness and mental illness were linked. According to Kirby, what began as a homeless project focused on the Downtown East Side in Vancouver "expanded into a project targeted at the homeless mental ill" in five Canadian cities, primarily "because of the Prime Minister's interest in dealing with people with mental illness" (p. 103). As this process unfolded (between 2007 and 2008), MacNaughton et al. observe that Kirby's "skills, resources, and access as an insider—both within the mental health movement . . . and within government" enabled him "to build broad-based support among the key decision-makers" (p. 104). They describe the process as a "rhetorical drama" (citing Greenhalgh & Russell, 2005) of "knowledge translation/exchange and evidence-based policy making" (p. 106) that brought about the initial conception of the At Home/Chez Soi study.

In 2008, the MHCC persuaded the federal government to provide $110 million to fund a five-year demonstration project (2009-2013), At Home/Chez Soi, that adopted an evidence-based research approach for five PHF demonstration projects. This approach (a) makes targeting the mentally ill and/or addicted, who make up a large segment of the "chronically and episodically homeless" population, attractive for its cost-effectiveness compared to costs for other homeless populations, and (b) embraces a collaborative research approach that includes non-traditional participants such as homelessness service-providers. The project was modelled on the original Pathways HF model, which "targeted ... chronically homeless people with severe mental health problems," many of whom "were reported to have also had . . . co-occurring substance misuse problems" (Tsemberis & Eisenberg, 2000 in Johnsen & Teixiera, 2012, p. 185). The *At Home/Chez Soi Interim Report* (2012) itself explicitly cites Pathways as its model:

Housing First is an evidence-based practice, originating in New York City (Pathways to Housing) in the 1990s and Toronto (Streets to Homes) in 2005, that provides immediate access to both permanent, independent housing and to mental health and support services. (Goering et al., September 2012, p. 8)

UPTAKE OF HF FROM ADVOCACY AND RESEARCH INTO GOVERNANCE (LEGISLATION)

In 2013, The Homeless Hub, a national source of homelessness policy and advocacy, reported on the costliness of traditional approaches to homelessness—"one that relies heavily on emergency services . . . a very expensive way of responding to a seemingly intractable problem" that entails costs for "shelters," "services," "health care," and "policing" (Cost Effectiveness of Ending Homelessness, p. 1). The report cites the *State of Homelessness in Canada 2013* report that estimates "the cumulative annual cost of our current approach is $7 billion dollars (p. 1). Of the research showing the cost-effectiveness of HF, the Homeless Hub cites the At Home/Chez Soi project as "the most compelling" showing "that implementing Housing First" is convincingly cost-effective compared to "treatment as usual" programs (p. 1). Another Homeless Hub report (2013) praises the At Home/Chez Soi study "as the world's largest and most-in-depth evidence-based exploration of the effectiveness of Housing First" (Gaetz, Scott, & Gulliver, p. 4).

The evidence-based approach adopted by the AH/CS team also involved a reconfigured collaborative approach to research, involving a wide range of participants—researchers, policy experts, government staff, and service-providers. This collaborative approach afforded a role for advocacy such that the Interim Report of the *At Home/Chez Soi* project shows the researchers negotiating their findings of cost-effectiveness with social justice priorities. On the one hand, the authors endorse the cost-effectiveness of a HF approach:

> Housing first makes better use of public dollars—especially for those who are high service users. (Goering et al., September 2012, p. 6)

On the other hand, they tie this benefit to the health and social well-being of homeless individuals:

> Of course, budgetary concerns need to be linked to the housing,
> health and social improvements that result from the Housing
> First programs. (p. 30)

This collaborative element was seen by project participants as critical to
political uptake. Collaboration was effective in both the early stage of
the project, which culminated in uptake enactments that transformed a
proposal into a funded pilot project (2008), and later in the run up to the
2013 budget, whereby uptake enactments from the *At Home/Chez Soi*
report became translated as HF budget criteria transforming the project
into a funded program. One of the AH/CS lead researchers, also an
advocate, described the importance of collaboration between researchers and policy experts as a strategy for influencing decision-making at
the highest level. Consciously adopting a "participatory" approach, they
used their access to the MHCC's intergovernmental office to promote
HF to the policy makers:

> They [Mental Health Commission of Canada] do have an in-
> tergovernmental office in the commission and we have worked
> very closely with members of that intergovernmental office
> [MHCC] throughout the project around how to position our-
> selves and communicate with government as we go along . . . it
> basically says if you want research to actually have uptake then
> you have to be very participatory throughout it. You can't wait
> until the end and then try to convince people to make decisions.
> (Interview, May 16/13)

This collaborative approach was deployed in tandem with the kairotic
strategy of anticipatory timing. They timed presenting their interim results to policy analysts and advocacy groups when the analysts were de-
ciding whether to turn the AH/CS project into a funded HF program.
By "shopping around on the hill ... all last summer," they managed to
influence government policy analysts just "as they were making decisions" about the program:

> . . . we put in place a very extensive intergovernmental commu-
> nications strategy that involved taking interim project results,
> which were available last September, and putting them in front
> of government . . . we were shopping around on the hill and in
> offices and in the government all last summer. So that they had
> results that they could see what we were learning as they were

making decisions about what they were going to do about—
what we call transition . . . away from a demonstration project
into programs. (Interview, May 16/13)

Collaboration between researchers, senior policy analysts, and advocacy
groups facilitated the kairotic coordination for presenting the cost-effective findings of the interim results to policy experts just as they were
deliberating over changes to the homelessness budget item, the Housing
Partnership Strategy (HPS).

> . . . in the process of trying to convince government to pick up
> some of the funding for the end of the project, I think what we
> did was actually get our findings and this housing first pro-
> gram and what we were learning much more on their agenda
> when they were thinking about what was going to happen to the
> Homeless Partnering Strategy [HPS] (Interview, May 16/13).

Moreover, aware of the power of advocates as part of this collaboration,
the researchers were "providing evidence to . . . advocacy groups . . . at
the same time" and were thus able to synchronize the timing with them
as well:

> We are obviously not the only ones talking to government. And
> part of the way I think science influences things is by provid-
> ing evidence to your advocacy groups who then use it in their
> conversations with government and that was also happening at
> the same time, we know that. (Interview, *At Home/Chez Soi* re-
> searcher, May 16/13)

In their elaboration of genre system theory, Yates and Orlikowsky (2002)
posit that a "genre system, as a series of genres, compris[es] a social activity [that is] enacted by all the parties involved," and thereby provides
"expectations" for "structuring the timing of coordinated social interaction" (104). This elaboration provides a genre-based explanation of how
strategic uptake, through kairotic opportunism and coordination, can
exploit the resources or affordances of genres in some sort of systemic
relationship. In the case of HF uptake from research into legislation,
it seems that researchers, policy analysts, and advocates coordinated
their respective genre systems through opportunistic timing (kairos)
and shared knowledge, and through this joint mediation they created
a strong nexus of relevant generic threads that paved the way to uptake
enactment.

The government-sponsored, evidence-based research genre, here instantiated by the *At Home/Chez Soi* interim report (2013) (and later by the final report (2014), functions as an "intermediary genre," a category proposed by Tachino (2012): "one genre can be used to connect and mobilize two otherwise unconnected genres to make uptake possible" (p. 456). Tachino (2013) ascribes two functions to this intermediary genre, knowledge-making and policy uptake, and explains that they are effects of the "coupling" of research and policy genres: it is a "coupling of form and content, and "language and power" across genres for the purpose of uptake by another genre (pp. 4-6). Tachino suggests that, "[if] coupling increases the probability of uptake, then the intermediary genre may be more effective by incorporating features of the target genres while preserving the aspects of the source genre that should be taken up" (p. 6). In the case of the *At Home/Chez Soi* interim report, features of advocacy in the form of social justice statements, and of economics in the form of evidence-based statements attesting to the cost-effectiveness of the HF approach, which would resonate with the fiscal priorities of a budget, the target genre, are incorporated into the intermediary genre, a research paper that elaborates and promotes the HF approach for its social justice objectives and its demonstrated social and economic effectiveness. Following Tachino's definition, the research report is a "primary" intermediary genre because researchers actively collaborated with the advocates and bureaucrats, and even coordinated a kairotic moment among them to ensure that the HF approach, which had been taken up from advocacy genres, was taken up by the budget. Since the research was funded by the federal government and clearly intended to be used for policy decisions, there was a direct link between research and governance, and another reason for designating such research as a primary intermediary genre. Further evidence of this function is the citation of the *At Home/ Chez Soi Interim Report* in the legislation itself:

> [Canada's] Economic Action Plan 2013 proposes $119 million per year over five years . . . to the Homelessness Partnering Strategy using a "Housing First" approach.

> The outcomes of the Mental Health Commission of Canada's *At Home/Chez Soi* Project have shown that providing *Housing First* . . . [is] an effective way to reduce homelessness. (Homelessness Partnering Strategy, Ch. 3.5: Supporting Families and Communities, *Budget 2013*, Government of Canada, March 21/13)

As Tachino (2012) argues, the popularity of such evidence-based research, where elements of policy are present in the research genre, attests to its generic transitioning or "re-purposing" towards wider recognition of the intermediary function and the status of a "primary" intermediary genre (pp. 460, 471).

It seems to many observers that the federal government's endorsement of HF for its effectiveness was as much or more for its cost-effectiveness. The primary monetary motivation for adopting HF budget criteria is explicit in a press release from the Mental Health Commission of Canada, who managed the Chez Soi project: "For highest service users, Housing First has proven particularly cost-effective with every $10 invested resulting in cost-savings of $21.72" (MHCC, April 9, 2014). Even before the Chez Soi study, several Canadian studies had already indicated that HF resulted in cost-savings. In 2012, a leading homelessness policy analyst in Canada, Stephen Gaetz, referred to seven such studies (2002-2010) that, in his view, provide "considerable evidence that Housing First approaches, even though they involve rent subsidies, and in some cases intensive case management, can save money" (p. 12). The *At Home/Chez Soi Interim Report* specifically reports that "[o]verall, for high service users [the chronically homeless], the annual cost savings . . . is $9,390 per person, per year" (Goering et al., 2012, p. 27).

The HF model was clearly attractive to the federal government for its evidence-based approach to research and policy making, which makes cost effectiveness a primary criterion: it foregrounds the economic advantages that fit with the policy priorities of many current western governments. In "The Curious Case of Housing First," Stanhope and Dunn (2011) explain the neoliberal ascendance of the influence of "economic models" on research and government's penchant for "market solutions," which they argue have helped precipitate governments' embracing of the HF model:

> The trend towards neoliberalism both in the United States and Europe have placed the market as the organizing force for resource allocation. . . . The resulting pervasive bias toward market solutions and the emergence of economic theory to inform research, has meant that economic models have shaped many aspects of research. . . . *Problems are framed in terms of costs and benefits.* (2011: 275-282, emphasis added)

Because mentally ill people are the most expensive to house, they became the targeted homeless population for HF. As Stanhope and Dunn (2011) elaborate, "Due to a series of landmark studies that identified the service use patterns of this subgroup, their particular contribution to the problem of homelessness was shown in stark relief" and "the costs were alarmingly high." With the "problem thus framed as chronic and expensive" (p. 277), the "business case" for targeting mentally ill populations was thus confirmed. As homelessness policy advocates, Stanhope and Dunn criticize the research for its exclusionary choice of this population as a "rational policy" choice that should instead, they argue, involve "a political debate about the ends—namely, who has a right to housing and how resources should be allocated among people experiencing homelessness" (p. 277). To reiterate a key factor that played an important role in the reception of the 2013 budget item, while the original "Pathways" HF model also targeted the "chronically and episodically homeless," it was never intended to exclude other homeless populations.

Additional uptake by news media reports (from both research and government press releases), a secondary intermediary genre whose primary purpose is to inform the public, tended to be mostly positive and may therefore have also contributed to the force of kairotic coordination towards HF uptake into the 2013 budget. Uptake by the media began to appear immediately after the *At Home/Chez Soi Interim Report* was published in September 2012. In the following examples, the HF At Home/Chez Soi approach is framed positively, as a significant breakthrough that may "reshape" how homelessness can be addressed, with the advantage of being cost-effective:

> The study's preliminary findings, to be released by the Mental Health Commission of Canada, show the potential value of an approach known as "housing first.". . . The findings could reshape the way governments and social services agencies in Canada and around the world tackle the challenge. . . . For the 10 per cent of participants who used the most services before the study began, the program saved government $9,390 a year. (Anne McIlroy, "Home, sweet home gives hope to mentally ill," *Globe & Mail*, Sept. 21/12, A4.)

> The thesis behind the $110-million study [*Chez Soi*]—run by the MHCC and funded by the federal government—is that participants would stabilize if given *housing first* and then support

services to address their challenges. . . . Preliminary findings by the academic researchers show those in the apartments are healthier and relied less on expensive crisis services like shelter, jails, and emergency rooms after just one year in their homes. (Lori Culbert, "It's 'almost like you've got friends'," *Vancouver Sun.*, Nov. 27/12, A8)

The three generic threads from advocacy, research, and government genres, subject to varying motivations, some cooperative (advocacy, research, and policy; research and government) and some potentially at odds (advocacy and government), became "jointly mediated" in the discursive event of the government's uptake of HF. A genre ecology of the relevant threads of this uptake includes advocacy policies, HSPs, OCPs, research studies of Pathways HF sites, Continuum of Care studies, the At Home/Chez Soi study, policy analyses of the At Home/Chez Soi results, fiscal policy of the federal government, and news media and other genres reporting on the At Home/Chez Soi results. The budget language, both its enabling and its restrictive dimensions, exists as a product of the degree to which these genres and participants could align themselves and their respective interests. In the following section, analysis shows how the particular uptake of HF by the government initially looked like a victory for advocates, but that, in reality, it constituted an unanticipated erosion of their values and social justice goals. As Freadman has emphasized, participants cannot secure an uptake of their choice: they can only strategize and anticipate.

UPTAKE OF HF FROM GOVERNANCE INTO ADVOCACY AND SERVICE-PROVISION

While within the homelessness genre system, researchers, advocates, and policy experts found the opportunity to persuade the federal government to enact the HF model as policy in the 2013 budget, findings show that the government seems to have deployed a strategy of rhetorical identification with advocacy, while at the same time compromising funding for key HF supports. This provoked an ambivalent reception. On the one hand, the government's HF model offered advocates a modicum of "rhetorical compensation" (Munro, 2007) through uptake from advocacy and research genres of shared language from the original "housing first" model, and so offered initial optimism among advocates about how it would work. On the other hand, it made service-provider agencies financially responsible for key supports, specifically health care and rent subsidies, which had been funded in the Chez Soi study and played a key role in the success of the study. Additionally, the legislation stipulated that HF projects must offer "barrier-free entry" and "housing choice," effectively ruling out current recovery houses. The overriding change, however, was the distribution of the HPS funds which, critically, shifted the funding formula to replace the traditional 100% devoted to services and shelters for a variety of homeless and people at-risk of homelessness with a formula that reassigned 65% of the fund to HF projects for the "chronically and episodically homeless," with the remaining 35% available for non-HF services.

The following sub-sections describe how advocates brought their historical understanding of HF to their uptake responses to the government's version of HF, vocalizing their strong awareness a) that HF projects would not receive sufficient funds to provide the full set of services and supports required to emulate the effective version of HF as established by the AH/CS research, and, b) that the stipulated restrictions for HF funding eligibility—the exclusive targeted population, HF entry criteria, and housing choice—posed challenges to the values and traditional practice of advocates and service-providers. The following analyses of this uptake by service-providers and advocates foregrounds the "notable absences" (Devitt, 2009, p. 34) in the government's budget policy, and the confusion and challenges it created for the advocacy and provider community. The evidence includes analysis of what Scroter (2013) broadly calls the "metadiscourse" or contextual evidence of these absences (pp. 47-60) in the "talk" of advocates and service providers (as recorded at meetings and in solicited interviews) whose consciousness and knowledge of the history of HF derives from their long genre memory and experience in the homelessness genre system. Theirs is a deep genre memory of activism and struggle and an attachment to the idea of HF as a "solution" to homelessness. It contrasts sharply with the more "shallow" genre memory of the federal government whose motivation was more rooted in the values and practices of evidence-based policy-making and economic conservatism.

Insufficient Funding for HF Projects

On the one hand, the pathway from research into policy genres seems well-worn, and, especially where research has been government-sponsored, the intermediary function of the research genre might seem routine. However, as Kertesz et al. (2009) caution in their study of HF policy, "the junction of scientific research and policy is fraught with risk." They emphasize that, "if findings are invoked incautiously or are applied beyond the limits of the original research, then 'overreach' will be the result. With overreach, outcomes may not correspond to projected benefits and risk the public's disenchantment" (pp. 497-498). The federal government's uptake of HF seems just such a case of "overreach"— the adoption of an apparently simple and effective intervention in the service-provider community that may have convinced some publics as a solution to homelessness, but that disrupted the homelessness service provider community. As Spinuzzi and Zachry (2000) argue, the "interconnections of genre" are contingent and uncertain: "contingency involves the complex, opportunistic, sometimes risky coordinations among genres that are made by people who are trying to accomplish certain things" (p. 173). In the government's enactment of HF uptake, the contingencies involved in the coordination of research, policy, and political and economic imperatives disrupted the advocacy and service-provider community and initiated subsequent uptakes that challenged and retranslated the government's version of HF.

Advocates in the homelessness genre system often have a decades' long "memory," and an archive of texts as evidence, of the altruistic motivations and the broader philosophy of HF, of the community's inclusive and social justice goals, and its experience of "struggle." From a genre system perspective, it seems the federal government, in contrast, had no such well-worn pathway in the system. Rather it had a "shallow" genre memory of the homelessness genre system that went back only as far as the AH/CS study and the finding of the evidence-based "cost-effectiveness" of its HF model. One long-time advocate expressed the community's criticism of the government's fiscal motivations ("they're very hard right on 'it's cheaper'") and apparent disinterest in other motivations ("not a shred of compassion"):

> . . . on the one hand, harm reduction is a compassionate, effective way of dealing with people who have severe addictions and mental health issues, but you can also make the economic case that it's cheaper to do HF. . . . So that's where the federal government comes in, they're very hard right on 'it's cheaper'. . . . There's not a shred of compassion whatsoever there, it's just going to be less expensive . . . they see this as a fiscally

effective alternative as proven by the At Home project. (Interview, April 20, 2015).

Another advocate, a project manager of an HF site that received federal funding under the new legislation, moved by her social justice values, cites a colleague who implicitly contrasts the government's HF funding criteria with the full funding of the At Home/Chez Soi study ("the Cadillac model") and argues that "every HF program" should have full funding:

> So [a colleague] actually said 'Everybody calls Chez Soi the Cadillac. Everybody talks about it as being you know, whatever, the best.' She says "I don't think it was the Cadillac. I think it was ... how it should be. Every [HF] program should be funded to that point.' (March 2, 2016).

Comments from another leader in the advocacy community also reflect the government's shallow memory of the HF model, which both advocates and the At Home/Chez Soi researchers understood requires funding for the critical support components of long-term rental supplements and health care to be successful. In an early interview, this informant, a long-time member of the Metro-Vancouver RSCH, pointed to the general underfunding of the HPS:

> . . . even our Metro proposal, which is coming up in Vancouver, in a few weeks, we are going to be issuing a call for letters of intent. We are going to have six million dollars to give out. For you know . . . six million, for the entire lower Van. So, I mean one project alone will cost six million dollars and that would be thirty units, right? So there's very little that we can do. So these people have to be prepared to be asking for a half a million dollars, a few hundred thousand dollars, and they got to get the rest of the money from somewhere else. (May 18, 2012)

In another interview three years later, this informant suggests the government may not understand the seriousness of omitting key AH/CS supports and how this will jeopardize the future success of the five AH/CS project sites, which were renewed under the new funding formula, but for only five years:

> . . . indeed, it could really be that the federal government was blind . . . did not recognize that At Home/Chez Soi was not

something that you could just transform into a federal program because it did not observe all those jurisdictional factors . . . it was a research project that . . .what they're saying is 'this is a time-limited program. After five years, there's no more money.' It sets them up for failure. (Interview, May 5, 2015).

She also pointed out "the absence of . . . money for rent supplements" and "clinical support" (May 5, 2015). Shortly after the budget was passed, this same advocate had been invited by the federal government to provide input on their HF model as part of an "experts" committee (The National Working Group on Housing First), members of which were sworn to secrecy. She describes her initial enthusiasm to participate in the process:

> . . . initially . . . I was really thrilled . . . I said 'They're creating a program based on evidence, isn't that amazing? Isn't that odd for the conservatives? They never do that. They do everything based on ideology. But . . . maybe things are changing.' I'm eternally optimistic. . . . I was applauding it. . . . And then they said, 'We don't know that much about how to implement this program, so we're going to bring together some experts from across the country,' and they included me in that, so I go to Ottawa. (Interview, May 5, 2015)

But this enthusiasm soon turned to the realization that the government would not be providing "rent supplements dollars" and "clinical support":

> and we start telling them 'this is what's needed in order to make HF work. You need to allow capital dollars . . . you need to have rent supplement dollars, you need to be able to provide clinical support. Those three things.' They went, 'No, we're not doing that.' (May 5, 2015).

Service providers also registered their concern over the lack of rent subsidies:

> . . . the only housing money we have access to if you are Housing First is for a maximum of three months and if that person's rent sub increases or whatever doesn't come through in that three months, Housing First claws back the money from you. (Executive Director of a Women's Shelter, April 19, 2016)

So, for example, criteria of Housing First is that you have the ability to have wrap-around services. You have to have clinicians on your team, they want you to have a nurse, nurses, or nurse practitioners. . . . Okay, so all those pieces. They wouldn't pay for any of that. (Regional Coordinator of a Women's Shelter, March 8, 2016)

As a result of the reduction in federal funds for services and shelters, some service providers had their federal funding completely cut off. For example, a safe house for youth, and a prevention program had their funding cut because of the new criteria:

Time has run out on the Iron Horse Youth Safe House. . . . The shelter's future has been uncertain for a year following a change in federal funding. Since it opened in 2005, the shelter has relied on the federal Homelessness Partnering Strategy to pay most of its $375,000 budget. But under the Housing First strategy announced a few years ago, 65 per cent of that money has to go to physical living spaces. ("Youth safe house ready to close," *Maple Ridge News,* Dec. 2/14).

Government funding cuts have put Sources Community Resource Centre's homelessness programs in jeopardy and left the non-profit organization scrambling to make up the difference. . . . Employment and Social Development Canada would cease funding Sources' Newton-based homeless prevention services, which since 2005 have helped more than 11,000 Sources clients . . . stay in their homes . . . the cuts have come as a result of the federal government initiating a new funding approach. ("Homelessness funding takes a hit," *Peace Arch News,* Jan. 13/15)

Stipulated Restrictions for HF Funding Eligibility

The government's version of HF also stood in contrast to the more robust version of homelessness support salient in the advocacy system, the model based on the social justice principle that housing is a human right, not only for the street homeless but for anyone at-risk of homelessness. As noted earlier, this principle is stated clearly by the developer of the original Pathways HF model: "Housing is a basic human right" (Tsemberis,

2010). Under the new budget criteria, the reduction in funding available for services for non-chronically homeless people profoundly affected the service-provider sector. As noted earlier, whereas pre-2013 at-risk populations were eligible for HPS funding for support services, whether HF or not, post-2013 non-HF service providers must compete for funding from an overall fund shrunk from 100% to 35% (with the other 65% dedicated to HF initiatives). The problem for service-providers has been that most services had, in response to previous criteria, been non-HF for there had been little or no funding dedicated to permanent housing. So, while the government reiterated the HF language of Pathways from the *Chez Soi* report, the loss of 65% of these funds and a widespread incapacity to be HF-ready (a costly undertaking that would require new capital) meant that in April 2015 most of the HPS funds were awarded to only a handful of HF initiatives, a situation one advocate who helped facilitate funding proposals described as "embarrassing" (Interview, April 30/15). In sum, the federal government's uptake of HF and its cost-effective motivation, based on the results of the AH/CS study, but with restrictive stipulations, disrupted the structures and delivery of homelessness services for a variety of homeless people including those at risk of homelessness.

Instead, the legislation and most of the HPS dollars explicitly targeted the "chronically and episodically homeless." When the federal government reiterated its 2014 announcement of $600 million over five years (2014-2019) "to renew and refocus the HPS (Homelessness Partnership Strategy) using a Housing First approach" (Press Release, updated May 14, 2015), it identified the target population as "those with mental illness," elaborated in the 2015 press release as "primarily individuals who are chronically or episodically homeless," who would be moved "from the streets of homeless shelters directly into permanent housing." The legislation setting out funding eligibility criteria for "[k]nowledge and capacity building in Housing First" again stipulated the target population as "the chronically and episodically homeless population" (Section 2.6 "Eligible Priorities and Activities," *Homelessness Partnering Strategy (HPS) 2014-2019*, Government of Canada, April 2014). HPS HF funding criteria does state the need to be inclusive of diverse populations (Aboriginals, women, the LGBT community, etc.), but HF criteria would only include them if they are also among the most visible, chronically homeless with a mental illness and/or addiction issue. The "Primary Population" checklist for applicants is as follows:

> Organizations that currently serve the chronically and/or ep-
> isodically homeless, preparing to serve the chronically and/or
> episodically homeless, that currently serve Aboriginal commu-
> nities, Women, Seniors, Youth, Official language minorities,
> Veterans, Families, LGBT community, people with disabilities,
> addictions, or mental illness. (Section 2.7, Sent to service pro-
> viders from the RSCH by email, April 4, 2014).

While HF uptake by the government was initially rhetorically effective
and lauded by advocates, the broader vision of HF as inclusive of those
at-risk of homelessness was at odds with the "primary population" targeted for funding. Advocates' memory of these other populations (Table 2)
who also needed assistance, perhaps services more than housing, was historically a key value and goal. The new HF criteria constituted a threat
to their ideology and social justice values and initially provoked criticism
and resistance to the power of the government.

As reported earlier, while the targeted population in the original Pathways projects was also "chronically homeless people with severe mental
health problems," many [with] . . . co-occurring substance misuse problems (Tsemberis & Eisenberg, 2000 in Johnsen & Teixiera, 2012, p.
185), advocates of Pathways never intended to exclude other homeless
populations from HF. The Pathways website now promotes housing as
a "right" for "everyone." Advocates saw that different homeless populations had different needs and thus would require tailored approaches to
services. And this approach is born out elsewhere by recent HF policy
that promotes diverse approaches responsive to local contexts and local
population needs, a shift that advocates became aware of and embraced.
However, for western governments, "the chronically homeless" have become the face of HF. The exclusionary effects of the HF emphasis on
the street homeless have been a concern among policy makers. Pleace, for
example, argues that HF "downplays the scale of homelessness":

> As the Housing First movement . . . spreads across the US and
> into the EU . . . taking centre-stage in strategic responses to
> homelessness, it brings with it a particular image of what 'home-
> lessness' is. That image is of a chaotic people with high sup-
> port needs, a subset of the much larger US homeless population
> that Continuum of Care staircase services and then PHF were
> specifically designed for. . . Emphasising the characteristics

of vulnerable individuals who present a minority of homeless people downplays the scale of homelessness. . . . (Pleace, 2011, p. 122)

In the first round of HF funding in 2014, most of the funds (65%) went to 16 HF projects for the "chronically or episodically homeless" and five capital projects to build housing for people who "are homeless or at imminent risk of homelessness," primarily for seniors and women, populations who have been traditionally supported. The remaining funds (35%) were awarded to 12 support services projects targeting people "at imminent risk" or "at risk of homelessness" (HPS MetroVancouver Region—Fiscal Year One Investment Report, Mar. 25/15), those other populations that figure so prominently in advocacy culture.

The reduction and, in some cases, elimination of funding of current services for at-risk populations became a key source of distress among service-providers, an anxiety of genre memory of the inclusive group of people who are at-risk of homelessness. The government's HF emphasis on the most visible, street homeless people with a mental illness or dual diagnosis is a conspicuous "presence" that throws into relief the notable reduction and sometimes "absence" of services for other at-risk populations. For advocates the logic of housing as a right entailed application to everyone.

> Importantly, PHF [Pathways Housing First] also regards housing to be a fundamental right, not something that should be earned or used to entice people into treatment or sobriety. (Johnsen & Teixeira, 2012)

> Housing First separates treatment from housing, considering the former voluntary and the latter a fundamental need and human right. (Johnsen & Teixiera, 2010)

The principle that housing is a right is implicit in the original Pathways model and has come to be an assumption in HF models. Having long held this inclusive understanding of approaches to homelessness, advocates in BC have reacted critically to the exclusionary effects of the federal government's version of the HF model. A "Constituent Member" of the RSCH criticized the government's HF criteria as too "restrictive" in terms of who would be eligible for help:

> . . . it's pretty restrictive to only creating housing for people who are really vulnerable and either homeless or having some kind of serious problem that's going to make them homeless imminently. So there's lots and lots of people who need afford-able housing, rental housing, and there's no funding for that . . . because they don't have addiction, they don't have mental ill-nesses, they're not being violent, they don't have a severe disabil-ity of any kind, so they actually wouldn't qualify for any of the housing that's being funded through the province or through the HPS program. (Interview, May 18, 2012)

One prominent activist pointed out that "episodically and chronically homeless people" make up "less than 20 percent of the population" and that the HPS HF criteria excludes a much larger group of people "at-risk" of homelessness:

> . . . for the HF the target population was chronically and epi-sodically homeless . . . and I think a lot of these organizations were probably dealing with homeless people who were either at risk or who were homeless and didn't meet the criteria . . . but at-risk was defined as being in imminent danger of losing your housing like within a month . . . in other words, it's going to happen, not just it might happen, it is going to happen . . . so even for the at-risk populations . . . we need support services for those people, . . . in fact . . . episodically and chronically home-less people [make up] less than 20% of the population. (Inter-view, April 20, 2015)

The reduction in available funding for these other "at-risk" populations created a huge obstacle for advocates and service providers who had worked hard to establish programs dedicated to these groups. Their val-ue of inclusivity, belief in housing as a right, and day-to-day service went deep and far back in time—these were the underpinnings of their sphere of activity in the homelessness genre system. It seemed to them that the government's version of HF would threaten to undo much that they had accomplished. The crossing of the government's uptake of HF into this sphere of activity had a huge destabilizing impact on its core members.

One manager of a service-provider expressed the fear that the HF funding model would waste federal money on those mentally ill people who don't need that level of services:

The Housing First piece? The criticisms I personally would have . . . as a provider . . . it's a very expensive way to house people who may not need that level of service. . . The majority of them can manage in existing resources. . . If you can get them into the mainstream resources that don't cost as much as the Housing First model, you don't need to put them into Housing First . . . I would see the majority of those [other populations] as not fitting in with what I know, as a service provider, as Housing First. (Interview, Nov. 18/13)

This manager's experience as an advocate and as a service provider working closely with homeless people gave her a first-hand experience of the different subpopulations of homeless and at-risk people. It was clear to her that the government, with its focus on "the chronically and episodically homeless" did not have this insider perspective and knowledge and couldn't appreciate the huge potential in helping these populations—they were resilient, likely able to become stably housed, and would likely cost less in the long run. These divergent understandings of the different needs of subpopulations of homeless people came into sharp focus as cross-purposes of two different genre systems, one with a history of working with the subpopulations and an ethic of inclusion, the other with a history of working with policy-makers and an ethic of cost-effectiveness.

The Director of two large recovery houses expressed concern that the HF funding model would displace some people now currently housed in shelters:

Housing first is an ideology which aims to deal with the hardest to house. Without more resources built, that will mean some shelters may have to go housing first ready. If they do that, then the current group of people in those shelters may be displaced to accommodate [they may] not feel safe in a housing first approach [sic]. (Email, April 21/14)

In 2013, at a HF workshop sponsored by Metro-Vancouver's Regional Steering Committee on Homelessness (RSCH), participants' input focused on the "other populations"—those people at-risk of homelessness who have traditionally turned to service-providers for help ("different populations," "the other groups," "the other population types," "women fleeing abuse," "newcomers," "seniors," "refugees," "aboriginal people," "youth," "not just people with mental health and/or addictions," "the hidden homeless"). The genre system, as Bakhtin might observe, remembered the "other populations" for them. The following comment is representative of this concern:

> Needs to be able to work for all population groups who are homeless, including youth, families, couples, single women, women fleeing abuse, people with disabilities, seniors, newcomers and refugees, Aboriginal people—as well as the hidden homeless.

Another participant cautions that HF addresses only "a very specific group" and is not therefore a panacea for homelessness:

> Beware trying to import the Housing First philosophy which was developed to address a very specific group of people experiencing street homelessness as the solution to all housing homelessness problems. (From minutes and report of a Metro Vancouver workshop held July 4/13, distributed Aug 12, 2013 by email)

The advocacy community came to interpret the funding changes as a violation of the principle of inclusiveness (which had become embedded, for example, in the expanding list of categories of homeless and at-risk people noted earlier in HPSs). Moreover, providers were keenly aware that the chronically homeless (the mentally ill and dual diagnosed) had always received priority for support services. This knowledge has often motivated service providers to seek ways to designate other at-risk populations as mentally ill. At a Strategic Planning Task Force meeting, one member explicitly referred to this practice:

> "There are certain places . . . where . . . the case managers simply kind of do it in such a way that . . . everybody who's homeless has a mental illness. . . . The point is they get the benefit. . . . That's the system, that's what happens in the real world, right?" (Nov. 29/11).

Many at the meeting conveyed nonverbal agreement with this practice. Providers deploy this tactic to resist government's restrictive criteria for eligibility for services so that they can maximize the number of people who become eligible—a response based on the advocacy community's value of inclusion. There is a degree of collusion or collaboration among providers and workers to work together toward this goal, and this is clearly a practice that has a history and consensus within the community. This is one way the marginal had been working the continuum-of-care system toward greater inclusivity, a way that would be less effective under the new funding criteria.

The exclusionary effects of the new budget criteria only heightened the perception that other needy at-risk populations were being left out. Advocates' responses to the budget attest to the salience and influence of shared genre memory. In a typical iteration, a leading Canadian advocate affirms that "everyone is deemed to be 'housing-ready'" and eligible for the full range of wrap-around services:

> "Housing First" has emerged as a key strategy in North America, the premise being that the best response to homelessness is to house people immediately (everyone is deemed to be "housing ready"), and then surround them with the kinds of supports they need (23). (Gaetz, Editorial, 2010, "The Struggle to End Homelessness in Canada: How We Created the Crisis, and How We Can End it, *The Open Health Services and Policy Journal*, Vol. 3, 2010: 21-26)

As residue in the homelessness genre system among advocates and service-providers, the "memory" of the principle of inclusivity, those other categories of homeless people, and long-held practices and tactics in the delivery of homeless services for both homeless and at-risk populations, converged with urgency in the wake of the budget. In the dynamics of a changed funding situation the exigencies of justice and equality for homeless people exerted an influence that was expressed as a persistent unease about the reductive effects of the 2013 budget. As advocates mobilized to develop strategies for building capacity toward eligibility for HF funding—however elusive that might seem for many service providers—their responses reflected a reluctant and resistant uptake with a number of criticisms of the exclusionary effects of the new criteria and funding formula. Later, those service providers whose HF funding proposals were successful were motivated by their concern for these other populations to work locally together to make up for budget shortcomings in their implementation of HPS HF programs. This long-standing collaborative practice is described later in this chapter. As an endemic practice in the advocacy community, collaborative strategies were deployed through an informal network to provide resources to make up for the funding shortfalls.

In addition to the restriction that government funded HF projects would target only the "chronically and episodically homeless," two other restrictions posed significant challenges for service-providers. First, funding activities tied to a HF model stipulate a "no barrier" principle for housing homeless people, but, as a licensing requirement, most recovery homes and shelters have barriers in the form of entry criteria. Many recovery houses and shelters were not eligible for funding because of their entry criteria, such as sobriety, which is a legal requirement for their license. In response to filling out a HF readiness survey, one service provider lamented their obvious ineligibility because of the no barrier principle:

> We operate three recovery houses for men, [unintelligible] houses. Uh I did the ... online survey thing for the housing first and . . . I would lose my certification under the assisted living register because I wouldn't have a program of recovery and I wouldn't have rules and responsibilities and so if that's what the housing first model is, it's f . . .'d. So. That's me. (Service provider, Task Force Meeting, Jan. 28/14).

Another challenge for service-providers was the federal government's incorporation of the HF principle that HF clients must be given a choice of housing type, location, and services. For many service providers, the scarcity of social and affordable housing and the problem of various unscrupulous landlords made the idea of "choice" a laughable ambition.

. . . .

Response to the new budget criteria was a mixture of fear, anxious efforts to interpret the federal version of HF, and urgent strategies in the advocacy community for building capacity for meeting the HF funding criteria. Instead of the solution that would "end homelessness" that so many providers had come to associate with the HF approach, they perceived the government's HF uptake in the funding criteria as a major rupture in the system, fraught with obstacles, for few of them were HF-ready and most had structured their services to fit the old criteria for both homeless and at-risk populations. At the outset, Metro-Vancouver's RSCH became involved initially conducting a HF readiness survey and then hosting HF capacity-building workshops. Advocates and service-providers already had a strong relationship and common vision, largely through their joint membership on homelessness task forces, and they immediately began to work together to address the new funding criteria. The challenge for advocates and service-providers was to interpret and conform to the federal government's definition of HF to qualify for funding under new 2013 HF criteria, and, at the same time, sustain an inclusive approach.

The nature of their collective genre "memory" is captured by Spinuzzi's insight (2003) that genre memory "represents others' 'thinking out' of problems whose dialogue has been preserved in the genre" (p. 43). In this case, the advocacy community has thought out and grappled with the complex problem of homelessness over decades of involvement. This genre residue includes the historical assumption of an inclusive homelessness philosophy and the practice of collaboration. Their uptake of the government's budgetary adoption of HF principles was "doubly oriented . . . toward *history* and *addressivity*" (Spinuzzi, 2003, p. 42, italics in original). As advocates respond, they heed their genre memory but also orient their strategy towards the government's version of HF to strategize for HF capacity-building.

The public was generally unaware of these ground-level problems with the government's HF funding criteria. In contrast to the advocacy community, news media uptake of HF was positive and unproblematized, emerging from a shallower genre memory than that of advocates, primarily based on reports of recent press releases and official announcements. An examination of the titles of articles from three Canadian newspapers between September 2012 and April 2014 that cite the phrase "housing first" showed that 26 of a total of 28 articles stage a positive and uncritical reception of the government's adoption of HF (see Table 5):

Table 5. Canadian News Articles on HF: September 2012 – April 2014

Globe and Mail	Ottawa Citizen	Vancouver Sun	TOTAL
6/7	8/8	12/13	26/28

Representative Examples of Titles:

- "Home, sweet home gives hope to mentally ill"
- "Study concludes 'housing first' works"
- "Housing first, fewer homeless later"
- "many jurisdictions have adopted a 'housing first' approach to homelessness, recognizing safe shelter as a prerequisite for a healthy, fruitful life"
- "'At Home' and thriving"
- "At Home: If this place wasn't here, I'd be dead"

- "Housing the homeless costs the same as leaving them in the cold: Final results of ... study reveal benefit of sheltering and supporting the mentally ill and drug addicted"

What the public heard was mostly a positive response to the government's budget for homeless people and not the consternation experienced by advocates and service-providers. Notably, the two negative news articles are framed as reported "warnings" from advocates who express concern about other homeless populations:

> "Ottawa's housing policy may be missing mark with youth, report warns"(*Van Sun*)

The second negative report cites American experts who are critical of the Canadian legislation for its exclusionary effects:

> Canada should not limit its new approach to homelessness to only people with mental illness or those who are perpetually on the streets, says a group of top U.S. experts with 10 years of experience in the field . . . they said the new strategy [housing-first] should be applied across the board, since it would benefit homeless people of all kinds—not just the subset of those with serious mental-health issues or who are frequently on the street or in shelters. ("Housing First plan limiting, U.S. experts warn," 2013)

In response, an acknowledgement is made by a Vice President of the federal funding body for the AH/CS study wherein he declares that "the concepts . . . are generalizable and applicable" to other at-risk populations. This AH/CS representative acknowledges the need to expand HF to other populations:

> Cameron Keller, a vice-president at the mental health commission [Canada]. . . doesn't see why it couldn't be applied more broadly. "I think the concepts, absolutely, are generalizable and applicable." (Heather Scoffield, "Canada's Housing First plan for homeless limiting, U.S. experts warn," *The Canadian Press*, Mar. 31/13, online; Heather Scoffield, "Housing First plan limiting, U.S. experts warn," *G & M*, April 1/13, A8)

At both the national and local levels of post-budget uptake, differences between government, news media, and advocacy uptake reveal different paths of uptake across different generic boundaries. HF uptake by governments has been described as an "evangelical" embracing of HF across North America and Europe (Johnsen & Teixiera, 2012). It recontextualizes HF in budget criteria based on a response to its cost-effectiveness, with little awareness of the priorities and principles arrived at over years of experience by advocates and service-providers. Both government and media have a "memory" of HF that is second-hand and based on others' reports—respectively, research reports and press releases. On the other hand, when HF uptake crosses the boundaries of research and government into the discourse of homelessness advocates it carries a residue of genre whose "memory" of HF is 30 years long and has often involved advocacy in the context of lived experience. The pathways of uptake in government and the news media result in shallower uptake, such that HF uptake in these genres is less moored to its antecedent generic contexts. Government's interests have a high fiscal priority, and the media has little at stake regarding HF. The data collected here strongly suggest that such shallow memory and reductive uptake help explain why the government's announcements, taken up by the news media, are generally more positive, unproblematized, and simplistic, and why advocacy uptake is more fraught, complex, and uneven. This positive uptake by government and media was widespread in both North America and Europe where it seems there had been a "wholesale 'conversion' to Housing First" (Johnsen and Tiexiera, 2012, p. 199).

The following section analyzes the textual and oral discourse pertaining to three different HF projects for comparative purposes—to focus on differences in funding sources and differences in implementation which show how local entities have strategized with HF criteria. The first, the Moncton site, received full funding as a participant in the AH/CS project that was renewed for five years; the second is a transitional shelter funded by several partners including the BC provincial government; and the third at Elizabeth Fry (EFry) has been funded partially by the federal HPS HF fund:

1. The Moncton Chez Soi demonstration project (the "pure" or "cadillac" version modelled on the Pathways model, fully HPS-HF funded, 2008-2013), now renewed for five years.

2. An unnamed transitional shelter in Greater Vancouver (partially provincially and federally funded, opened in 2015).

3. Two Elizabeth Fry shelters in Greater Vancouver (partially HPS-HF funded, opened in 2015).

Within the generic sphere of activity of homelessness advocacy, service-providers have improvised uptake of HF in their efforts towards creating successful HF projects. As noted, two key features of this activity come into play as evocations of participants' genre memory: 1) their shared social justice values of human rights and inclusiveness, through which they have developed a shared consciousness and historical understanding of their advocacy experience and goals, and 2) their historical practices of collaboration through support networks and collective action.

These values, understandings, and practices are activated as resources for a strategic response to the exigencies of inclusiveness and the task of negotiating the HF budget criteria with a shortage of funds and services towards realizing the actual construction and material reality of homes for the homeless at locally adapted sites. Uptake again crosses generic boundaries from the federal definition of HF in legislation back into advocacy. The following shows how the key values and practices of the advocacy community come into play in their uptake of the HF approach and are mobilized in the implementation of HF sites.

Social Justice Values and HF: Rights and Inclusiveness

The primary social justice values among participants in homelessness advocacy are inclusiveness and action for social justice and the belief that housing is a human right. A report on the Moncton Chez Soi HF project captures both:

> Housing First is an innovative approach to working with homeless people premised on the notion that housing is a basic human right, and therefore should not be denied to anyone ("Evaluating ... a Demonstration Project: At Home/Chez Soi Moncton," Flowers, Gaucher, & Bourque, 2014, p. 8).

The operations manager of the federally funded transition shelter echoed this understanding:

> the idea that housing is, is a human right. . . . Housing and health are Canadian human rights. . . . So I think maybe that is one of the driving values as I see that they are the rights of Canadian citizens. . . . that is sort of the core value there. . . . Our core

value statement is that there is a home for everyone. (Operations Manager, transitional shelter, April 23/16)

Embedded in advocates' "rights" discourse are the values of equality, inclusiveness, and care—the strongly held belief that all homeless people, including those at risk of homelessness, have a right to a home, not just the PHF target population of "chronically and episodically homeless" people, and that all are deserving of human compassion. As the context for HF has changed over time, specifically the values and consciousness of participants in the genre system of which it is a key feature, the long memory of its association with social justice and equality has motivated service-providers to advocate for HF for all homeless populations.

As noted in my discussion of an earlier stage of their HF uptake, advocates have expressed their concern that some homeless populations are entirely excluded. Policy experts and academics have now been re-assessing HF in this light. Klodawsky (2009), a policy researcher, suggests that instead of "concentrating scarce resources on a hard-to-serve population" resources could "structurally addre[ss] the adverse impacts of too little affordable housing for a much broader marginalized population" (p. 602). Other policy analysts and researchers echo this concern, especially noting the exclusion of "women and families" from HF programs:

> HF-type programs are . . . frequently . . . targeted, however, at a particular category of people. . . . Researchers, advocates, and service providers have pointed out that the construction of and focus on the label of "chronic homelessness" can draw attention away from the homelessness of those who do not fit the category . . . [and] in Canada could obscure the visibility of women and families who are homeless, and therefore divert funding away from programs for these groups. (Katz, Zerger, & Hwang, 2016, p. 2)

Similarly, a report by a campaign for housing for women, registers concern that the hidden homeless, particularly "women and girls," are automatically excluded from HF programs:

> Precisely because the homelessness of women and girls is more likely to be hidden, there is concern that many will be categorically excluded from eligibility for Housing First programs. Inclusion criteria for Housing First models for those experiencing chronic homelessness need reflect an appreciation of the

gendered nature of experiences of homelessness. (*Housing First, Women Second?*, 2013, p. 4).

The yoking of advocacy and support for women at-risk with the HF approach is enshrined in the rights philosophy of Elizabeth Fry (EFry). The Executive Director describes E Fry as a "human rights organization" based on "feminist values," an orientation that makes the agency's primary goal "change management":

> We only take those programs on where we see it is a human rights issue. . . . We define ourselves as a human rights organization first off . . . because rights come first in the work. . . . If you are a human rights organization your job is change management. (Executive Director, E Fry, April 19/16)

She points out that the government's funding criteria excludes ex-offenders with PTSD, and, by extension, the children of ex-offenders who have been diagnosed with PTSD. The ACT team she refers to is a key component of HF support yet is restricted to working with only certain populations:

> Women are not served by ACT [HF Assertive Community Treatment] teams because ACT teams will not take you if you have an access to diagnosis. So anybody who has PTSD. You can be a schizophrenic with PTSD and they will not take you because of the PTSD diagnosis. . . . So some of those definitions don't work, for women. They are blind to children. . . . It won't pay your transportation as a mother to get your child to school to register them in school and take them to school. (Executive Director, April 19/16)

Such concerns with lack of inclusiveness have been widespread among advocates and service providers. For example, at the Moncton Chez Soi site, inclusiveness became an ethical issue because of the research design. Concerns about exclusion resulted in two radical changes to the Chez Soi Moncton project in its initial planning stages. First, members of the planning committee redesigned their study when they realized that important sectors of their homelessness populations in the city would have been excluded from eligibility for the HF project in the original design:

> The project's initial design would have excluded the following: those living temporarily with friends or families; those in

transition; those temporarily without a dwelling; and those living in long-term institutions . . . The discordance between the stereotypical vision of homelessness [street homeless] and the local reality [primarily at-risk populations] was problematic in the planning phase. (Flowers, Gaucher, & Bourque, 2014, pp. 11-12)

Second, because the project stipulated a "treatment-as-usual" (TAU) control group who would be excluded from receiving HF supports, the original research team (which included advocates and service-providers) withdrew from the project:

> Actors began questioning the ethics of recruiting potential participants [for TAU], offering hope with regard to bettering their situation only to return half of it back to inadequate living arrangements and long waiting lists for mental health services. . . . The chosen methodology was among the reasons for which the original research team withdrew from the project: . . . Members of the research team to follow were equally troubled: "I mean nobody wants to turn anyone down. You're not the one that wants to say you've been randomized to care as usual." (p. 14)

Clearly, values associated with social justice and inclusion came into conflict with HF in terms of eligibility for HF funding and HF research. However, while these community values led to acts of resistance, the community's practice and ethos of collaboration helped realize productive strategies for filling in the gaps in services because of insufficient HF funding. As Klodawsky (2009) points out, for advocates the basic motivation behind Housing First derives more from "economies of care" than the "formal market economy" (p. 594). This shared ethic of care is captured in a comment by the chair of one task force that helped manage the transitional shelter HF project:

> I see the right to housing being maybe at the structural level but I think it is the human values around, . . . meeting the needs of people who are obviously stressed. To me I think that is the core requirement, and I think that is what always drove the task force. (Task Force Chair, Apr. 23/16)

A Collaborative Ethos and Practice

Collaboration and mutual support have long been indispensable to the culture of "community organizing" and was a vital practice in the homelessness sphere of activity. As Pare (2014) notes in his review of genre theory and rhetorical agency, in the post-modern context of reduced "personal freedom from regulation," where the individual actor has dubious agency, individuals adopt "collective strategies . . . to act effectively and collaboratively within the structures of a community." Pare thus negotiates the question of individual agency, asserting that "agency is something we exercise *with others,* rather than alone" (pp. A-89-90). Such collective agency characterizes the successful implementation of HF by service-providers working with insufficient resources. As with many advocacy groups, in the genre system of homelessness advocacy, collaboration has been a valued practice for decades. It has become a central networking strategy in the prevalent genre of "10 year plans to end homelessness" and is visible today in the composition of municipal homelessness task forces, which typically includes representatives from a number of service providers, housing societies, landlords, law enforcement, health authorities, and municipal governments.

Not surprisingly, the federal government has seen opportunity in these collaborative practices within the homelessness community. They are a cost-reducing resource for the federal government, which *requires* HPS projects to draw upon existing supports and partners to provide those HF supports not covered by federal funding, especially "clinical services":

> The collaboration of service providers who provide these supports [housing, clinical, and complementary supports] is strongly encouraged and expected. The HF approach requires collaborative service delivery to ensure that persons . . . receive the supports they need. . . . Housing, clinical and complementary service providers would work together to serve all of the needs of the individual. . . . Communities are . . . strongly encouraged to link up with existing clinical services. (Housing First Supports, HPS, Employment and Social Development Canada, 2016, pp. 2-3)

In response to this requirement, HF implementers have mobilized their existing networks of providers. The Canadian Alliance for Ending

Homelessness articulates the importance of this traditional practice of collaboration in moving forward with the "new" HF model:

> Those who were already working in the housing system in Vancouver, who believed in a new approach to homelessness (including the Housing First model) and who had *compassion, empathy, and patience,* were sought to develop and implement the program. This also helped to keep *the collaborative spirit* behind what was being created. (HF Case Studies, The Homeless Hub, 2015, p. 6, emphasis added)

This is a clarion call to the homelessness community to remember its values and its collaborative underpinnings.

As indicated, an important participant in advocacy's collaborative practices is the Metro-Vancouver RSCH, the regional constituency that has been delegated to adjudicate and award successful HPS-HF proposals in British Columbia It helps service providers meet the government's criteria for HF funding by hosting workshops to help organizations "map the services that are available in the [cities] to support implementation of Housing First programs in [the] community" as "part of an HPS-funded program" (April 24/16). The Steering Committee has held several workshops and assisted service-providers with their HF funding proposals. Many members of the RSCH have been working together on the front lines of homelessness for years. They include policy analysts, service-providers, outreach workers, police and health authority representatives, city planners, social housing experts, and formerly homeless people.

HF project managers also mobilized local networks of service providers to make up for unfunded services. At EFry, the Regional Manager explained that, given the government's "criteria of Housing First is that you [must] have the ability to have wrap around services," the agency activated existing relationships with social service agencies whose "workers were then educated to refer [clients] to Housing First." She added that, while "this was the outreach work, . . . on our list, that became a financial contribution [in their expense reports for the government]." She described this network building as a "huge undertaking," but one that "is working actually. . . . It is just the resourcefulness of non-profits really" (Mar. 8/16). She cited an example that illustrates how collaboration works at the micro-level of practice, in which she describes how a working group of outreach workers coordinates supports and housing for clients. In this example, a woman, "Diane," has appeared at one agency in the network and "is looking pretty rough":

> [the outreach workers] took out a working group amongst them, where they . . . know who is working with whom mainly. But let's say the Front Room sees you know Diane at the Front Room and they know [another organization] has been working with them . . . or whatever they have been working collaboratively with them, to get them housed, and they might call and say, "oh I thought you just housed Diane last week, and she is here at the Front Room, and she is looking pretty rough." Right. So they will call and then the worker might come, or the Lookout worker might actually engage them and say, "Here is a bus ticket, so and so is over there. Why don't you go see them?" . . . It is powerful. (Regional Manager, HF, EFry, Mar. 8/16)

For the Surrey site, EFry partnered with three key social service organizations and a network of approximately 16 service providers and teams. The New Westminster site has a different network profile, which includes two women's prisons, police agencies, probation professionals, a hospital, and landlords.

At the transitional shelter for the street homeless, which was funded by several partners including the BC provincial government (not HPS), and opened in December 2015, partnerships and networks were also activated to achieve a reasonable facsimile of the HF model. A community organizer involved in the establishment of this shelter reports that "the cooperation component is still growing." He predicted that the "facility will continue to grow as a hub with more and more services, either with services provided here or with strong connections to services available" (Task Force Chair, April 23/16). The collaborative network for this site has been comprehensive. Funding partners include, among others, the city (who provided the land), the provincial government, and a housing society that finances the building site and staff. Service providers and other community supports include two health authorities, a mental health agency, at least five other shelters/services (a dental clinic and an on-site nurse are to come), the homelessness task force, law professionals, faith organizations, and three municipal governments.

At the Moncton AH/CS project, the history of collaboration among local advocates and service-providers no doubt contributed to a conflict that developed between researchers and local advocates. It is possible that, because the Chez Soi sites were fully funded, there was less incentive among researchers to tap into pre-existing relationships to save costs and, therefore, less interest in mobilizing historical community practices. The Moncton project was largely run by researchers for the MHCC and not local providers. Collaboration seemed to be less valued by government implementers and became a significant issue for several team members, who felt their participation as advocates and local knowledge-keepers had been minimalized:

> Despite the fact that a variety of individuals were consulted, few besides the site coordinator were involved in the overall planning and development of the project. . . . One key player clearly stated that participation in the process was fragmented, meaning that most players' contribution was limited to a small portion of the process. . . . The majority of key players ultimately did not see themselves as such. (Flowers, Gaucher, & Bourque, 2014, pp. 12-13)

To remain faithful to the social justice goals of homelessness advocacy and to negotiate the challenges of a scarcity of funds and resources, HF implementers critically depend on collaboration and pre-existing networks of support. The municipal homelessness task forces, which are comprehensively representative of this network, seem to be structurally at the centre of the genre system and sphere of activity of homelessness advocacy and provide the strongest and most adaptable fusing of form (HF), substance (values and practices), and situation (local HF sites). Unlike macro-collaborations, such as coalitions and alliances, such networks of collective actors are attached to a cultural sphere of activity, localized homelessness advocacy, and exist at "the threshold of genre" (Giltrow, 2016, p. 66). This explains why, at the Moncton site, where protocols from the research system crossed over into the homelessness advocacy sphere of activity, they collided with the values of inclusiveness and collaboration. As noted, advocates also expressed concerns that the TAU participants would be excluded from treatment: "The chosen methodology was among the reasons for which the original research team withdrew from the project" (Flowers, Gaucher, & Bourque, 2014, p. 14). It seems that discomfort among local advocates and providers was an expression of a sense of boundary violation and genre disorientation. In effect, at the Moncton site, the research team seems to have been disconnected from the deep local memory of the advocacy community, so that the research genre came to colonize advocacy instead of engaging it.

Implementers' uptake enactments of HF and their concomitant actions accomplish genre's pragmatic force through the creation of unique operational HF sites. Historically rooted, collective uptake sets priorities for how the PHF model is interpreted locally. For example, echoing the "cadillac" analogy, the task force chair describes how their transitional "hf" shelter (a "harm reduction" program) differs, in a positive way, from the PHF model (for the "hard-to-house"), calling theirs lower case "hf" as opposed to capitalized "HF":

> I think there is a difference, in my mind. Housing First capital 'H' capital 'F'. My understanding is it was specifically a paradigm for dealing with people who are hard-to-house. The idea there was that . . . they are going to be there permanently . . . forever. That is their place. . . . I think that housing first—small 'h' small 'f'—it is really just . . . a harm reduction program. So you bring someone in, provide them shelter without barriers, and then you attend to their needs and provide support services. . . . People with transitional housing typically aren't thinking . . . this as permanent housing. . . . So to me, it is the harm reduction principles applied to housing. So I call it small 'h', small 'f' housing. (Task Force Chair, April 23/16).

The Operations Manager at this site was even more emphatic about the differences, contrasting the At Home/Chez Soi project and their HF transitional shelter as "like day and night" (April 23/16). In practice, each HF site fulfills HF criteria approximately because full criteria are either unattainable or not desirable.

As we have seen, the challenge of meeting the government's full criteria for HF funding and implementation initially disturbed and destabilized the homelessness service-provider sphere of activity, yet it also activated their network to collaborate to develop creative strategies to nevertheless qualify for HF funding. In turn, their efforts began to re-stabilize the system of homelessness advocacy and care, acceding to the governance genre system, yet still striving to meet key advocacy goals of social justice. This involved a careful translation of HF uptake into different instantiations of HF, many of which were lower case "hf." In other words, both the de-stabilizing and re-stabilizing effects of genre are at play: uptake of the federal criteria for HF funding disturbs the service-provider and advocacy community yet activates its existing re-sources such that each unique deployment of the HF model, the ac-complishment of generic social action, manifests as an adaptation of the unattainable "pure" version. In this sense, most HF sites may be viewed as lower case "hf" versions, each with different combinations of tran-sitional or permanent housing, and varying support services. In each project, as uptake crosses boundaries from governance into advocacy, a dialogical translation is negotiated involving the selection of generic threads of both central, official genres controlling funding and the more unofficial, marginal genres of advocacy whose practices and values re-translate HF into a local facsimile of housing and services. As the evolv-ing understandings of HF in the advocacy community negotiate HF funding shortages and different levels of need among client populations, as these generic threads from advocacy are "jointly mediated" with those of higher-level genres of governance, HF becomes recontextualized and accommodated in advocacy contexts, stabilizing the genre "for now." This mediation draws together diverse generic threads to form a nexus that "provisionally" restabilizes the homelessness genre system and the advocacy community whose "sphere of activity" carries on its construc-tive practices of remediation.

Genre theory and the concept of uptake offer insights for how the short-sightedness and fiscal priorities can negatively impact the intended recipients of assistance, and for how social justice advocacy communities deploy tactics to resist yet capitalize on the disturbances of a more domi-nant power by activating the traditional tools and practices of their com-munity. Such cycles of fraught uptakes (small victories?) may perhaps be what constitute the process of enduring struggles for social justice.

5 Conclusion

This analysis of uptake of HF by government and the translation of this uptake by the homelessness advocacy community has implications for both HF and for our understanding of the relationship between genre and uptake in the crossing of genre boundaries, and as both destabilizing and stabilizing forces.

HOUSING FIRST

The analysis helps to explain why the HF approach is now undergoing change and why a variety of HF interpretations have subsequently been offered for different populations and needs. The dynamics of the government's uptake of HF and the genre memory that became activated as advocates "remembered" other homeless populations, seem to corroborate recent criticism of "pure" HF approaches that target only the chronically homeless. Policy experts now question "whether the policy and research focus on Housing First is overemphasizing one aspect of the wider social problem of homelessness" (Pleace, 2011, p.113). As noted, some now argue that most homeless people do not fit the original PHF profile of chronically homeless people with mental illness and/or addiction issues, and that in most cases other larger socio-economic issues are driving homelessness (Pleace, 2011, pp. 122-123). Significantly, the Jury of the EU Consensus Conference endorses, not a HF approach, but a "housing-led" model that addresses "all forms of homelessness":

> . . . 'housing-led' [is] a broader, differentiated concept encompassing approaches that aim to provide housing, with support as required, as the initial step in addressing all forms of homelessness. 'Housing-led' thus encompasses the 'Housing First' model as part of a broader group of policy approaches" (Pleace & Bretherton, n.d., p. 14 on p.6).

In effect, the "paradigm shift" in Canada, from the government's previous continuum of care and housing to a HF model, is giving way elsewhere to "paradigm drift" (Pleace & Bretherton) whereby serious consideration is given to alternative variants of the Pathways HF model and is defined in "terms of a *range* of services" (p. 13). As Pleace and Bretherton observe, "as Housing First has permeated the thinking of policymakers and service providers across the US and the wider world, the PHF service model has often been simplified, diluted and in many instances, subjected to significant change" (2012, p. 5). As discussed in an earlier section, in Kertesz et al.'s (2009) overview of studies of HF and continuum of care or staircase models, they raise "a cautionary note" in terms of possible HF "overreach" by governments. They report that "similar cautionary notes were raised by a German permanent supportive housing study in which severe substance abuse reduced housing tenure . . . and by a Philadelphia study reporting substance abuse by 47 percent of persons whose departure from housing was characterized prospectively as 'voluntary'" (p. 505). They also note other studies that report "not all the supportive housing approaches were pure Housing First approaches" (p. 505).

These variants of the original Pathways HF project are a response to the need to adapt HF to local populations and contexts, and a challenge to its exclusionary emphasis. In the cases of the two post-At Home/ Chez Soi HF sites analyzed here, as one advocate stated, the capital "HF" intervention is more of a lower case "hf" intervention, such that HF interventions can be offered, unproblematically, alongside recovery interventions within the same agency. At another HF site (not discussed in this monograph), the Executive Director of a homelessness service provider in Portland, Oregon blogs that his agency offers "Recovery Housing as well as Housing First supported housing programs." The HF program is "low-barrier" while in the Recovery Housing program "the use of alcohol and the unlawful use of drugs . . . is prohibited" (Blackburn, July 12, 2016, p. 1). Once again, the mandate and values of HF advocates are pushing back against the dominance of the government sanctioned HF model, paving the way toward more inclusive variants.

The reassessment of HF was a key subject of the 2016 European Research Conference on Homelessness. While there was a consensus that "We are in the housing first era" and that "Housing First is the national policy in Canada and the United States" and "in many countries in Europe," there was also an acknowledgement that the "pure" Pathways version is not required. One researcher pointed out that there is "no contradiction between running shelters or Housing First programmes in Denmark" where "the Housing First strategy is supported by social workers in shelters too" (International Network of Street Papers website, Oct. 28, 2016). These critiques and adaptations are not just the result of disinterested research. The context for both the research and policy are tied historically to advocacy and the genre memory of the community of homelessness advocates who challenge what they see as a lack of inclusivity, among other problems, in the "pure" version of HF. Even where well-intentioned, this problematic version seems to clearly be an effect of uptake informed by only a shallow genre memory of advocacy and insufficient participant history in the homelessness genre system.

UPTAKE AND GENRE

The analysis of the discursive chain of HF uptake enactments builds upon current theorizing of uptake and shows the productivity of a rhetorical genre framework for tracing both routine and disruptive uptake pathways in contexts of asymmetrical power relations and the dynamics of enduring struggles. In applying uptake and genre theory to an analysis of HF uptake, I have attempted to explain the different dynamics of uptake at the junctures of different genre boundaries. This has involved descriptions of the dynamics of HF uptake into lower level genres of policy (HSPs) which were relatively non-problematic, of HF uptake into research from advocacy and policy which became enacted more serendipitously, of HF uptake from research into governance which became disruptive, and of HF uptake from governance back into advocacy and implementation which triggered both resistant and constructive responses, actualizing genre memory as an antidote to disruptive uptake. These descriptions are offered as an elaboration of Tachino (2016, 2010) and Spinuzzi and Zachry's proposal (2003) for how uptake enactment occurs. Particularly relevant to the genre/uptake relationship, the analyses show disturbing effects within the less powerful advocacy community as government, a dominant power, enacts HF uptake. The results of the analyses distinguish between shallow, fossilized genre memory and deep, active genre memory, a distinction somewhat parallel to Giltrow's distinction between shared and unshared consciousness (2016). A shallow, fossilized genre memory lies behind uptakes of "form only," that is, form without the historical context of a consciousness passed down through time and experience to present-day participants (whether First Nations people, as in Giltrow's study, or advocates for the homeless in this one). The distinction is also related to Freadman's (2002) implied distinction between form with process and "form without process," the latter a "pastiche" that "serves the purpose of confirming the disempowerment of one jurisdiction and the power of the other" (p. 47) (whether a parody as in Freadman's "mimicry of a courtroom exchange" by a politician, or the calculated "overreach" of the federal government in the case of HF). Such uptake enactments of "form only" can have disruptive effects, such as those described in the wake of the government's uptake of the HF model and funding criteria.

Despite the disrupting effects of HF uptake analyzed here, as the dominant genre of governance colonizes research and advocacy, the uptake genre restabilizes, and the asymmetry in power relations is held intact by the effects of uptake enactment—the joint mediation of genre threads from government, advocacy, and research. Different generic threads, some compatible, others in conflict with each other, are drawn together from diverse genres, each with their own "interests," motivations and strategies driving the uptake event. The analyses demonstrate that, as uptake selection and enactment take place, the threads interact as a nexus and become temporarily reconfigured and recontextualized in the uptake genre. In turn, as the advocacy community takes up the government's HF criteria, they negotiate the problematic threads from legislation toward the re-establishment of another kind of stability in the advocacy community. While HF uptake from governance is imposed, it is not only restrictive, but also enabling with affordances. These opportunities are construed by advocates as means for both resisting and accommodating the imposition of the full HF model in their responses to funding applications and in their local realizations of "hf" projects.

The concepts of uptake and genre memory, anchored within a rhetorical genre framework reveal how participants in homelessness advocacy detect notable presences and absences of uptake, how genre residue and memory permeate the life of a genre, with both disruptive and constructive effects, and how, even in enactments of social change and resistance, the advocacy genre system can participate productively with a dominant power. In this way, an enduring struggle can reconstitute itself (Holland and Lave, 2001) where uptake, proffered by the less powerful and adopted by the more powerful, may be incomplete or problematic, where genre memory and residue are salient and notable, especially where the powerful lay claim rhetorically to the proffered uptake but carry out some "other" social action. In the case of HF and the struggle for homeless people, where shallow uptake from a less powerful genre by a dominant player into a higher official genre disturbs a community, the genre system furnishes subsequent and more elaborate uptake affordances from the deep well of advocates' genre memory as they attempt to reconstruct what has been textually silenced. It may be that the very existence of genre residue in the homelessness system presages the emergence of some form of residue uptake.[2] This might explain, in part, how it is that advocates hope and persist in contexts of enduring struggles.

I hope this study shows the usefulness of analyzing uptake as a genre-based phenomenon, specifically illustrating:

- uptake as multiple, contingent, and jointly mediated;
- genre-crossing as a dialogical encounter of past and present; and
- genre memory as deep or shallow.

In this study, a framework making these concepts central suggests a preliminary typology of uptake according to its effects—non-problematic, disruptive, and constructive. This is but one case of an enduring struggle, and it would be useful to examine other struggles such as the struggle for the environment, land, and equality through a genre/uptake lens to see if the distinctions and role of genre memory and the proposed typology of uptake found in the struggle for the homeless are replicated in other contexts.

The sequence of analyses of HF uptake enactments provides some insight into the struggle for homeless people: it involves what Holland and Lave describe as "active engagement" in "moving struggles" and suggests how such struggle seems to be "reconstituted." In their study of diverse but historically persistent struggles for social justice, Holland and Lave (2001) assert that such struggles are "long-term traditions shared by those joined in opposition" where "'answers' to 'addresses' made by the contentious other are authored in the cultural discourses and practices at hand" (pp. 23-30). The analyses here of HF uptake as a series of joint mediations between government and advocacy demonstrate how discourse reinscribes their relations of power as each answers the other in ways that are genre'd to hold their power relations in place, yet also to move the struggle forward slowly and incrementally.

---

2. Tosh Tachino (private communication, July 23/13)

References

Austin, J.L. (1962/1975), *How to do things with words.* Harvard University Press.

Bakhtin, M. (1986). The problem of speech genres. In C. Emerson & M. Holquist, *Speech genres and other late essays* (V. W. McGee, Trans.). University of Texas Press.

Bakhtin, M. (1963). *Problems of Dostoevsky's Poetics.* (Caryl Emerson, Ed. and Trans.). University of Minnesota Press.

Bawarshi, A. (2016a). Accounting for genre performances: why uptake matters. In N. Artemeva & A. Freedman (Eds.), *Genre studies around the globe: beyond three traditions* (pp. 186-206). Inkshed Publications, Trafford Publishing.

Bawarshi, A. (2016b). Between genres: Uptake, memory, and US public discourse on Israel- Palestine. In M. Reiff and A. Bawarshi (Eds.), *Genre and the Performance of Publics* (pp. 43-59). Utah State University Press.

Bawarshi, A. (2012). Rethinking genre through uptake: agency and innovation in rhetorical genre studies. Genre 2012 Conference (paper), Ottawa.

Bazerman, C. (1994). Systems of genres and the enactment of social intentions. In Freedman, A., & Medway, P. (Eds.), *Genre and the new rhetoric* (pp. 79–104). Taylor & Francis.

Berkenkotter, C., & Hanganu-Bresch, C. (2011). Occult genres and the certification of madness in a 19th-century lunatic asylum. *Written Communication, 28*(2), 220–250.

Bhatia, V. (2004). *Worlds of written discourse.* Continuum.

Blackburn, E. (July 12, 2016). Housing options lead to better outcomes. NAEH. www.endhomelessness.org.

Bitzer, L. (1968). The rhetorical situation. *Philosophy and Rhetoric, 1,* 1-14.

Canadian Alliance to End Homelessness. (2000). *A Plan, Not a Dream.*

Culbert, L. (Nov. 27, 2012). It's 'almost like you've got friends.' *Vancouver Sun,* A8.

Devitt, A. (1991). Intertextuality in tax accounting: Generic, referential, and functional. In C. Bazerman, J. Paradis (Eds.), *Textual dynamics of the professions* (pp. 336–357), University of Wisconsin Press.

Devitt, A. (2009). Re-fusing form in genre study. In J. Giltrow & D. Stein (Eds.), *Genres in the internet* (pp. 27–48), John Benjamins Publishing Company.

Dryer, D. (2016). Disambiguating uptake: Toward a tactical research agenda on citizens' writing. In M. Reiff and A. Bawarshi (Eds.), *Genre and the Performance of Publics* (pp. 60-79). Utah State University Press.

Dryer, D. (2012). Central problems in uptake studies: An assessment and two proposals. Ottawa: Genre 2012 Conference (paper).

Emmons, K. (2009). Uptake and the biomedical subject. In C. Bazerman, A. Bonini, & D. Figueiredo (Eds.), *Genre in a changing world* (pp. 134–157). Parlor Press.

Federation of Canadian Municipalities. (2008). *Sustaining the Momentum: Recommendations for a National Action Plan on Housing and Homelessness.*

Flowers, L., Gaucher, C., & Bourque J. (2014). Evaluating the planning and development phase of a demonstration project: At Home/Chez Soi Moncton. *Canadian Journal of Community Mental Health, 33*(4), 7-21.

Foucault, M. (1972). The discourse on language. Appendix to *The archaeology of knowledge* (A.M. Sheridan Smith, Trans.), (pp. 215-238). Pantheon Books.

Freadman, A. (1987, 1994). Anyone for tennis? In P. Medway and A. Freedman (Eds.), *Genre and the new rhetoric* (pp. 43-66). Taylor & Francis.

Freadman, A. (2002). *Uptake.* In R. Coe, L. Lingard, & T. Teslenko (Eds.), *The Rhetoric and ideology of genre* (pp. 39–56). Hampton Press.

Freadman, A. (2002). The invention of genres. *Canadian Review of Comparative Literature 29*(2–3), 343–376.

Freadman, A. (2012). The traps and trappings of genre theory. *Applied Linguistics, 33*(5), 544 –563.

Frow, J. (2006). *Genre.* Routledge.

Gaetz, S., Scott, F., & Gulliver, T. (Eds.) (2013). *Housing First in Canada: Supporting Communities to End Homelessness.* Canadian Homelessness Research Network Press.

Gaeetz, S. (2012). *The real cost of homelessness: Can we save money by doing the right thing?* Canadian Homelessness Research Network Press.

Gaetz, S. (2010). The struggle to end homelessness in Canada: How we created the crisis, and how we can end it (editorial). *The Open Health Services and Policy Journal, 3,* 21-26.

Giltrow, J. (2016). Bridging to genre: Spanning technological change. Forthcoming.

Giltrow, J. (2016). Form alone: The supreme court of Canada reading historical treaties. In N. Artemeva & A. Freedman (Eds.), *Genre studies around the globe: beyond three traditions* (pp. 207-224). Inkshed Publications, Trafford Publishing.

Giltrow, J. & Stein, D. (2009). Genres in the internet: innovation, evolution, and genre theory. In J. Giltrow & D. Stein (Eds.), *Genres in the internet* (pp. 1–26). John Benjamins Publishing Company.

Goering, P., et al. (2012). *At Home/Chez Soi interim report.* Mental Health Commission of Canada.

Goering, P., et al. (2014). *National final report: Cross-Site At Home/Chez Soi project.* Mental Health Commission of Canada.

Government of Canada. (2013). Homelessness partnering strategy, Ch. 3.5: Supporting families and communities. *Budget 2013.*

Holland, D., & Lave, J. (2001). History in person: an introduction. In D. Holland & J. Lave (Eds.), *History in person: Enduring struggles, contentious practice, intimate identities* (pp. 3-33). School of American Research Press.

Holquist M., & Emerson, C. (1981). Glossary. *The Dialogic Imagination: four essays by M.M. Bakhtin.* University of Texas Press.

HPS Metro Vancouver region—fiscal year one investment report. (March 25, 2015).

Housing first, women second? Gendering housing first. A Brief from the Homes for Women Campaign. October 28, 2013. Janet Mosher worked on the brief.

Huckin, T. (2002). Textual silence and the discourse of homelessness. *Discourse and society, 13*(3), 347–372.

Hyland, K. (1999). Academic attribution, citation and the construction of disciplinary knowledge. *Applied Linguistics, 20*(3), 341-367.

Hyland, K. (2009). Writing in the disciplines: Research evidence for specificity. *Taiwan International ESP Journal, 1,* 1: 5-22.

Johnsen, S., & Teixiera, L. (2012). 'Doing it already?': Stakeholder perceptions of housing first in the U.K. *International Journal of Housing Policy, 12*(2), 183–203.

Johnsen, S., & Teixiera, L. (2010). *Staircases, elevators and cycles of change: 'Housing first' and other housing models for homeless people with complex support needs.* Crisis (charity) and The Centre for Housing Policy at the University of York.

Katz, S., Zerger, S., & Hwang, S. (2017). Housing first the conversation: discourse, policy and the limits of the possible. *Critical Public Health, 27*(1), 1–7.

Kertesz, S.G., Crouch, K., Milby, J.B., Cusimano, R.E, & Schumacher, J.E. (2009). Housing first for homeless persons with active addiction: are we overreaching? *The Milbank Quarterly, 87*(2), 495–534.

Klodawsky, F. (2009). Home spaces and rights to the city: Thinking social justice for chronically homeless women. *Urban Geography, 30*(6), 591–610.

Macnaughton, E., Nelson, G., & Goering, P. (2013). Bringing politics and evidence together: Policy entrepreneurship and the conception of the At Home/Chez Soi Housing First Initiative for addressing homelessness and mental illness in Canada. *Social Science & Medicine, 82,* 100–107.

McIlroy, A. (Sept. 21, 2012). Home, sweet home gives hope to mentally ill. *Globe and Mail,* A4.

Metro-Vancouver Regional Steering Committee on Homelessness (website).

Miller, C. (1984). Genre as social action. *Quarterly Journal of Speech, 70,* 157–178.

Morson, G., & Emerson, C. (1990). Theory of genres. In G. Morson, C. & Emerson, C. (Eds.), *Mikhail Bakhtin: Creation of a prosaics* (pp. 271-305). Stanford University Press.

Munro, A. (2007). The Belsunce case judgment, uptake, genre. *Cultural Studies Review, 13*(2), 190–204.

Padgett, D.K. (2013.) Choices, consequences and context: Housing First and its critics. *European Journal of Homelesssness, 7*(2), 341–346.

Pare, A. (2014). Rhetorical genre theory and academic literacy. *Journal of Academic Language & Learning, 8*(1), A-83-A-94.

Pleace, N. (2011). The ambiguities, limits and risks of housing first from a European perspective.*European Journal of Homelessness, 5*(2): 113-127.

Pleace, N., & Bretherton, J. (2012). What do we mean by housing first? Categorising and critically assessing the housing first movement from a European perspective. ENHR Conference, Lillehammer, WS-14: Welfare Policy, Homelessness and Exclusion.

Pleace, N., & Bretherton, J. (n.d.). *Will paradigm drift stop housing first from ending homelessness? Categorising and critically assessing the housing first movement from a social policy perspective.* Centre for Housing Policy, University of York.

Rossall, P. (2011). News media representations of homelessness: Do economic news production pressures prevent journalists from adequately reporting complex social issues. *Ejournalist.com.au, 11*(2), 96-124.

Schiff, J. (2012). *Housing First.* Ottawa: Conference of the Federation of Canadian Municipalities.

Schneider,B., Chamberlain, K., & Hodgetts, D. (2010). Representations of homelessness in four Canadian newspapers: Regulation, control, and social order. *Journal of Sociology & Social Welfare, 37*(4), 147-172.

Schroter, M. (2013). *Silence and concealment in political discourse.* John Benjamins Publishing Company.

Schryer, C. (1993). Records as genre. *Written Communication, 10*(2), 200–234.

Scoffiels, H. (April 1, 2013). Housing first plan limiting, U.S. experts warn. *Globe and Mail,* A8.

Spinuzzi, C., & Zachry, M. (2000). Genre ecologies: An open-system approach to understanding and constructing documentation. *ACM Journal of Computer Documentation, 24*(3), 169-181.

Spinuzzi, C. (2003). *Tracing genres through organizations: A sociocultural approach to information design.* The MIT Press.

Tachino, T. (2016). Multiple intertextual threads and (un)likely uptakes: An analysis of a Canadian public inquiry. In M. Reiff & A. Bawarshi (Eds.), *Genre and the performance of publics* (pp. 178–198). Utah State University.

Tachino, T. (2013). Uptake and intermediary genre: further exploration. Victoria: Conference of the Canadian Association for the Study of Discourse and Writing (paper). Conference.

Tachino, T. (2012). Theorizing uptake and knowledge mobilization: A case for intermediary genre. *Written Communication, 29*(4), 455–476.

Tachino, T. (2010). Genre, ideology, and knowledge in academic research and public policy. *Linguagem em (Dis)curso, Palhoca, SC. 10*(3), 595–618.

Tsemberis, S. (2010). *Housing first: The pathways model to end homelessness for people with mental illness and addiction.* Hazelden.org

Tsemberis, S., & Asmussen, S. (1999). From streets to homes: The Pathways to Housing consumer preference supported housing model, *Alcoholism Treatment Quarterly, 17,* 113–131.

Union of B.C. Municipalities. (2008). *Policy Paper #2, Affordable Housing and Homelessness Strategy.*

Waegemakers Schiff, J., & Rook, J. (2012). *Housing first—where is the evidence?* The Homeless Hub.

Yates, J., & Orlikowski, W. (2002). Genre systems: Chronos and kairos in communicative interaction. In R. Coe, L. Lingard, & T. Teslenko, (Eds.), *The Rhetoric and ideology of genre* (pp 39–56). Hampton Press.

Appendix

HOUSING AND HOMELESSNESS STRATEGIC PLANS (HSPS)

City of Campbell River Homelessness Task Force Report,
    September 2009
Responding to Housing and Homelessness Needs: An Affordable
    Housing Strategy for the City of Chilliwack, September 2008
Kamloops Homelessness Action Plan, November 2011
Nanaimo's Response to Homelessness Action Plan, 2008
Masterplan for Housing the Homeless in Surrey, July 2013
Vancouver's Housing and Homelessness Strategy, 2012
Kelowna Housing Strategy, March 2012
Homelessness Action Strategy and Implementation Plan for New
    Westminster, December 2006
The Regional Homelessness Plan for Greater Vancouver, August 2005
Mayor's Task Force on Breaking the Cycle of Mental Illness,
    Addictions and Homelessness: Report of the Steering Committee,
    Victoria, October 2007

OFFICIAL COMMUNITY PLANS (OCPs) IN 2014

White Rock, September 2008
Port Moody, 2011
Victoria, 2012
New Westminster, 2011
North Peace Fringe Area, 2009
Surrey, 2013
Chilliwack, 1998
Whistler, 2011
Port Coquitlam, 2013
Campbell River, 2012
Kamloops, 2013
Pitt Meadows, 2007
Abbotsford, 2003
Coquitlam, 2004

About the Author

Diana Wegner taught in Arts Studies in Research and Writing at the University of British Columbia (2012-2019) and is a faculty emerita (Professional Writing Program, English, and Communications) at Douglas College, New Westminster, BC. She has also taught at Simon Fraser University (academic writing and research) and in the Faculty of Education (language studies) at the University of British Columbia. She continues to pursue scholarship in the analysis and theory of language and power in contexts of social struggle (environmentalism, homelessness, and Indigenous women's rights). She has also studied the dynamics of transitional writing as students move from the classroom to the professional workplace. Her work has been published in the *Journal of Business and Technical Communication, Rhetor,* the *Canadian Journal for the Study of Discourse,* and *Writing* (formerly *Technostyle*) and in edited collections on language and communication.

Photograph of the Author by the University of British Columbia. Used by permission.

www.ingramcontent.com/pod-product-compliance
Lightning Source LLC
Chambersburg PA
CBHW021625270326
41931CB00008B/867